THE U.S. NAVAL INSTITUTE ON

NAVAL
COMMAND

U.S. NAVAL INSTITUTE
WHEEL BOOKS

In the U.S. Navy, "Wheel Books" were once found in the uniform pockets of every junior and many senior petty officers. Each small notebook was unique to the Sailor carrying it, but all had in common a collection of data and wisdom that the individual deemed useful in the effective execution of his or her duties. Often used as a substitute for experience among neophytes and as a portable library of reference information for more experienced personnel, those weathered pages contained everything from the time of the next tide, to leadership hints from a respected chief petty officer, to the color coding of the phone-and-distance line used in underway replenishments.

In that same tradition, U.S. Naval Institute Wheel Books provide supplemental information, pragmatic advice, and cogent analysis on topics important to all naval professionals. Drawn from the U.S. Naval Institute's vast archives, the series combines articles from the Institute's flagship publication *Proceedings*, as well as selections from the oral history collection and from Naval Institute Press books, to create unique guides on a wide array of fundamental professional subjects.

THE U.S. NAVAL INSTITUTE ON

NAVAL COMMAND

EDITED BY THOMAS J. CUTLER

NAVAL INSTITUTE PRESS
Annapolis, Maryland

Naval Institute Press
291 Wood Road
Annapolis, MD 21402

Library of Congress Cataloging-in-Publication Data
The U.S. Naval Institute on naval command / edited by Thomas J. Cutler.
  pages cm. — (U.S. Naval Institute wheel books)
  Includes index.
  ISBN 978-1-61251-800-8 (pbk. : alk. paper) — ISBN 978-1-61251-889-3 (ebook)
1. United States. Navy—Officers' handbooks 2. Leadership—United States. 3.
Command of troops—United States. I. Cutler, Thomas J., 1947–, editor of compilation.
  V133.U84 2015
  359.3'30410973—dc23
                                                        2014046401

♾ Print editions meet the requirements of ANSI/NISO z39.48–1992
(Permanence of Paper). Printed in the United States of America.

23 22 21 20 19 18 17 16 15   9 8 7 6 5 4 3 2 1
First printing

CONTENTS

EDITOR'S NOTE

Because this book is an anthology, containing documents from different time periods, the selections included here are subject to varying styles and conventions. Other variables are introduced by the evolving nature of the Naval Institute's publication practices. For those reasons, certain editorial decisions were required in order to avoid introducing confusion or inconsistencies and to expedite the process of assembling these sometimes disparate pieces.

Gender

Most jarring of the differences that readers will encounter are likely those associated with gender. Many of the included selections were written when the armed forces were primarily a male domain and so adhere to purely masculine references. I have chosen to leave the original language intact in these documents for the sake of authenticity and to avoid the complications that can arise when trying to make anachronistic adjustments. So readers are asked to "translate" (converting the ubiquitous "he" to "he or she" and "his" to "her or his" as required) and, while doing so, to celebrate the progress that we have made in these matters in more recent times.

Author "Biographies"

Another problem arises when considering biographical information of the various authors whose works make up this special collection. Some of the selections included in this anthology were originally accompanied by biographical information about their authors. Others were not. Those "biographies" that do exist vary a great deal in terms of length and depth, some amounting to a single sentence pertaining to the author's current duty station, others consisting of several paragraphs that cover the author's career. Varying degrees of research—some quite time consuming and some yielding no results—are required to find biographical information from other sources. Because of these uneven variables, and because as a general rule we are more interested in what these authors have to say more than who they are or were, I have chosen to even the playing field by foregoing accompanying "biographies." Relevant biographical information has been included in some of the accompanying commentaries, however.

Ranks

I have retained the ranks of the authors *at the time of their publication.* Some authors wrote early in their careers, and the sagacity of their earlier contributions says much about the individuals, about the significance of the Naval Institute's forum, and about the importance of writing to the naval services—something that is sometimes under-appreciated.

Deletions

Most of the articles included here are intact, appearing as they originally did in their entirety, but in a few cases some portions have been removed because they make suggestions or challenge policies/programs that no longer exist. Where these deletions have occurred, the following has been inserted: [...]

In the interest of space, and because *Wheel Books* are intended as professional guides, not academic treatises, most citations have been removed.

Other Anomalies

Readers may detect some inconsistencies in editorial style, reflecting staff changes at the Naval Institute, evolving practices in publishing itself, and various other factors not always identifiable. Some of the selections will include citational support, others will not. Authors sometimes coined their own words and occasionally violated traditional style conventions. *Bottom line:* with the exception of the removal of some extraneous materials (such as section numbers from book excerpts) and the conversion to a consistent font and overall design, these articles and excerpts appear as they originally did when first published.

INTRODUCTION

When we first conceived of this "Wheel Book" series, we determined that an obvious choice for one of the first books would be one on leadership. As we reviewed the many articles on that subject that have appeared in Naval Institute publications over the years, it became apparent that we had many more possibilities than could fit into one reasonably sized volume. We also observed that many of the articles seemed to fit into another related but more specialized category—that of command.

What is command and how does it differ from leadership? While an exact definition that covers all the nuances and variations is not easily achieved, a somewhat simplistic but effective means of distinguishing between these two closely related elements is to consider leadership as leading individuals, while command is leading leaders.

While that distinction served us reasonably well as a guidepost in our selection process for the two volumes, it of course does not entirely capture all that the word "command" conjures. *The Dictionary of Naval Terms* (Naval Institute Press, 2005) defines command as "authority vested in an individual for the direction, coordination, and control of military forces." That is certainly true, but that definition does not fully embrace the essence of the word, the near-reverence that is often embedded in the term. Leaders are vitally important to organizations, both civilian and military, but commanders are something above and beyond mere leaders and are both unique and essential to military organizations.

1

That special essence is further complicated when the words "at sea" are appended. While this book will explore command in its purely military sense, it will come as no surprise that some emphasis will be given to that specialty within a specialty, command at sea. Joseph Conrad famously defined command at sea as "prestige, privilege, and burden," calling it "the most difficult and demanding assignment in the Navy" and "a duty which richly deserves the highest, time-honored title of the seafaring world." Indeed, in the opening selection of this book, Admiral Jim Stavridis quotes Conrad and follows his model by first explaining the prestige and privilege of command and then quickly making clear the accountability (burden) that comes with it.

It is also noteworthy that in his iconic book *Command at Sea*, Admiral Stavridis focuses on a theme that is notably ubiquitous in these pages, that of the independence of the commander. Perhaps it is a reflection of the American character—born in a revolution against monarchy and sustained through a necessarily independent frontier spirit—that brings this theme to prominence. Or perhaps it has its roots in that special situation encountered by captains of ships at sea. Most likely it is a combination of the two but, whatever its origins, the autonomy of commanders is often mentioned, frequently stressed, and almost always defended strongly.

It is important to note that it is autonomy—not autocracy—that is at issue here. These are not calls for excessive authority—in fact, rarely is the degree of authority over subordinates in question. It is the degree of interference from above that is most often at issue. Time and again, the call for more trust and less direction ("rudder orders") from superior officers emerges in these pages.

Commanders—actual and would-be—understand the need for a chain of command. The roles of policy, doctrine, and timely command and control are recognized and advocated. And it is generally understood that advances in technology and newly emerging priorities necessitate the evolution of the command relationship. But it is the manner and degree of these things, juxtaposed with the prerogatives of command, that are the primary bones of contention.

There is also recognition that there are obvious risks in the granting and preservation of autonomy, but the proposed remedy for that possibility is most often a call for greater scrutiny of the selection process rather than a lessening of authority or an increase in oversight.

In an August 1963 *Proceedings* article, Secretary of the Navy Fred Korth proposed an arguably optimal formula as "positive centralized direction, decentralized execution, and common doctrine and management by exception." But that is not the final word on the subject. Variations on that theme are the grist for a number of thought-provoking pieces that appear in these pages.

Other themes that emerge from these pages include the recognition of the delicate but enormously important balance between authority and responsibility, the differences that exist at various levels of command, and the very different challenges that face war-time and peace-time commanders.

As with other "Wheel Books" the potential corpus far exceeds the space available for a reasonably sized book. Many other articles or excerpts could easily have been included, and in an ideal world would be. Consequently, readers are urged to consider this anthology as but an "hors d'oeuvre" to the much more satisfying "meal" that is provided for those who have discovered the ongoing intellectual sustenance provided by the U.S. Naval Institute for the last one hundred and forty-two years . . . and for many more to come.

1 "TAKING COMMAND"

(Selection from chapter 1 of *Command at Sea*)

ADM James Stavridis, USN, and RDML Robert Girrier, USN

It is altogether appropriate that this collection should begin with an excerpt from the iconic guide *Command at Sea*. This venerable book has been authored through several editions by an impressive array of leaders/writers and has long been the source of advice and a handy reference for those who aspire to or are in command. This excerpt is taken from the latest (sixth) edition and is a portion of the opening chapter, in which Admirals Stavridis and Girrier introduce the subject and establish some of its parameters.

"TAKING COMMAND"

(Selection from chapter 1 of *Command at Sea, 6th Edition*) by ADM James Stavridis, USN, and RDML Robert Girrier, USN (Naval Institute Press, 2010): 1–8.

The experience of command of a ship at sea is unforgettable; it is without parallel or equal. The responsibility is heavy, but the rewards—which become embedded in the very fabric of your life—are priceless. The captain of the U.S. Navy warship stands as part of a long, unbroken line that stretches from the very founders of the Continental Navy through the great captains of America's wars at sea and on to the next generation of twenty-first-century leaders.

U.S. Navy Regulations, fully updated last in 1990, states that "the responsibility of the commanding officer for his or her command is absolute" and that "the authority of the commanding officer is commensurate with his or her responsibility." These are simple, clear, binding statements. No amount of explanation can alter their placement of ultimate responsibility—whether for success or failure—squarely on the shoulders of the captain in command.

In this respect, though the size of a ship may be important as a measure of her capability, durability, and endurance, the smallest mine countermeasure ship or coastal patrol boat is equal to the largest aircraft carrier in terms of responsibility and reward. The commanding officers of both are "captains," regardless of the number of stripes they wear on their sleeves. Each must ensure the safety of the ship and crew, as well as the accomplishment of all assigned missions. Likewise, the skipper of an aircraft squadron assumes full and complete responsibility for the performance of a command at sea. *U.S. Navy Regulations,* in its chapter addressing commanding officers (0801), continues further, "In addition to commanding officers, the provisions of this chapter shall apply, where pertinent, to aircraft commanders, officers in charge (including warrant officers and petty officers when so detailed) and those persons standing the command duty."

Some thoughts from serving type commanders, from both Commander Naval Air Forces and Commander Naval Surface Forces, who have seen scores of commanding officers lead their ships through myriad challenges, provide valuable insight into what makes a successful CO.

Good COs can successfully translate policies to each individual in their command. They take care of their crew's well being, ensuring they attend the right professional schools, are trained properly for their jobs, and take time for leave as appropriate. They provide opportunities and a development path for their crew members. They are the chief morale officer for their shipmates and their families too. A good CO builds cohesion, afloat and ashore. Part of professional growth is the process of instilling high standards. Successful COs clearly articulate and enforce these standards in all areas: personal conduct, professional performance, material readiness, rigorous training, and especially, crisp execution. They teach customs and traditions. Successful COs follow up, inspect, and hold crew members accountable in a disciplined manner. They provide feedback up and down the chain of command.

As COs become more senior, commanding larger vessels with crews from 2,500 to 3,000 personnel, their scope of responsibility naturally increases. In these larger ships more seasoned subordinates will serve, and successful COs adjust their leadership style to this reality. The most successful COs increasingly empower their subordinates as the size of their command grows. This requires good communication skills and the ability to connect in a broad context with the whole command, as well as with each specific department and division. Successful COs are true professional experts within their commands—they lead from the air, and they lead from the bridge. They continuously teach and mentor. The crew must see this, as it reinforces the CO's credibility. Good COs are "out and about" as a matter of routine. They know their ship, and they know the environment. The crew will see this too, and this "full contact" approach will build trust.

Certain red flags mark an unsuccessful CO's behavior and consistently signal trouble. COs who fail to delegate responsibility and hold individuals accountable, or who lead solely from their staterooms via a continuous stream of e-mails will almost certainly flounder. When dialog between the CO and the crew becomes constrained, failure looms. Poor material readiness, low cleanliness standards, and lack of attention in the correction of deficiencies are telltale signs of a command's failing health.

To achieve success in command, the captain must work through those whom he or she leads; little can be accomplished alone, no matter how brilliant one's individual talents. Admiral Chester Nimitz, on the occasion of a call by several of his captains, said, "Commanding a ship is the simplest task in the world, even if at times it seems complicated. A captain has only to pick good courses of action and to stick to them no matter what. If he is good and generally makes good decisions, his crew will cover for him if he fails occasionally. If he is bad, this fact will soon be known, and he must be removed with the speed of light."

The successful commanding officer, then, must learn to become as one with his or her wardroom and crew and to truly know their strengths and weaknesses; yet, at the same time, he or she must remain above and apart. This unique relationship has been the subject of study and story for centuries. It changes, yet it is timeless. It is a skill to be mastered in turn by each commander.

Two days prior to the Battle of Java Sea, in which HMS *Exeter* would be sunk in the dark early days of World War II in the Pacific, her commanding officer, Captain O. L. Gordon, Royal Navy, was having a late-evening drink at a Surabaya hotel with a group of young British and American junior officers. One of the American officers asked him how he felt about going to sea the next morning to meet the approaching Japanese naval force. Gordon knew that his ship would have little chance of surviving, but he smiled anyway as he said, "I would not trade all the Queen's jewels for the privilege of commanding *Exeter* tomorrow. I have the finest group of men ever to man a ship of war. They will not fail me, and they know I will not fail my Sovereign. We may not survive, but we will leave our mark." When the battle began, the gigantic battle ensign flown by the ship was an inspiration to the Allied ships that accompanied her. They knew she would be commanded well, and therefore would fight well.

Even the realm of literature is full of allusion to the art of command. Perhaps the best-known and most frequently quoted commentary on command at sea was written by Joseph Conrad, a writer who had himself commanded at sea as a merchant sailor:

The Prestige, Privilege and the Burden of Command

Only a seaman realizes to what extent an entire ship reflects the personality and ability of one individual, her Commanding Officer. To a landsman this is not understandable, and sometimes it is even difficult for us to comprehend,—but it is so.

A ship at sea is a distant world in herself and in consideration of the protracted and distant operations of the fleet units the Navy must place great power, responsibility and trust in the hands of those leaders chosen for command.

In each ship there is one man who, in the hour of emergency or peril at sea, can turn to no other man. There is one who alone is ultimately responsible for the safe navigation, engineering performance, accurate gunfiring and morale of his ship. He is the Commanding Officer. He is the ship.

This is the most difficult and demanding assignment in the Navy. There is not an instant during his tour of duty as Commanding Officer that he can escape the grasp of command responsibility. His privileges in view of his obligations are most ludicrously small; nevertheless command is the spur which has given the Navy its great leaders.

It is a duty which most richly deserves the highest, time-honored title of the seafaring world—"CAPTAIN."

Conrad's thoughts on command are echoed by one of fiction's great captains, Jack Aubrey of Patrick O'Brian's superb series of sea novels about the nineteenth-century Royal Navy. Captain Aubrey's command philosophy is stated in a few sentences that are worth bearing in mind: "His idea of a crack ship was one with a strong, highly-skilled crew that could out-maneuver and then outshoot the opponent, a taut but happy ship, an efficient man-of-war—in short a ship that was likely to win at any reasonable odds."

A great deal has been written about command at sea over the years, but perhaps the thought that best sums up this most fulfilling assignment comes from another classic of sea literature, *The Caine Mutiny*. In it, Herman Wouk's immortal character Lieutenant Keefer expressed it well: "You can't understand command till you've had it." And once you have had command, you are changed forever, marked as one who has stood in the long line of captains at sea.

The Accountability of Command

In navies in general, and in the U.S. Navy in particular, strict accountability is an integral part of command. Not even the profession of medicine embraces the absolute accountability found at sea. A doctor may lose a patient under trying circumstances and continue to practice, but a naval officer seldom has the opportunity to hazard a second ship.

There have been, at times, those who question the strict and undeviating application of accountability in the Navy, but those who have been to sea have always closed ranks against the doubters. In 1952, for example, the destroyer *Hobson* collided with the aircraft carrier *Melbourne* during night flight operations. Damage was extensive, and the loss of life was heavy. There were extenuating circumstances, but in May 1952 the *Wall Street Journal*, in a frequently quoted discussion of the disaster, concluded:

> On the sea, there is a tradition older than the traditions of the country itself—it is the tradition that with responsibility goes authority and with them both goes accountability.
>
> It is cruel, this accountability of good and well intentioned men. But the choice is that or an end to responsibility and finally, as the cruel sea has taught, an end to the confidence and trust in the men who lead. For men will not long trust leaders who feel themselves beyond accountability for what they do.

The enormous significance of this responsibility and accountability for the lives and careers of others—and often the outcome of great issues as well—is the reason for the liberality of orders to officers commanding ships of the U.S. Navy. The inexperienced officer may erroneously take this liberality to reflect vagueness or indecision on the part of superiors. Nothing could be further from the truth. It is provided to give the commander the flexibility necessary to carry out his or her orders.

One incident in the 1970s led ultimately to a reinforcement of the doctrine of the absolute accountability of command. The incident began with the collision of the USS *Belknap* and the USS *John F. Kennedy*, in which the *Belknap* lost eight men and suffered $100 million in damages. The court-martial that followed caused many naval officers to reconsider the issues surrounding accountability of commanding officers. The Chief of Naval Operations, Admiral J. L. Holloway III, issued a memorandum dated 2 October 1976 discussing the entire issue. In subsequent years, several additional cases of groundings, collisions, and fires at sea have further emphasized the complete accountability of the commanding officer for the actions of the ship. Of note in this regard—and worth reviewing with the wardroom on occasion—are the grounding of USS *Spruance* in the Caribbean in 1989, the collision of the USS *Kinkaid* with a merchant tanker in the Straits of Malaga in 1991, the collision of the aircraft carrier USS *Theodore Roosevelt* with the cruiser *Leyte Gulf* in 1997, the fire aboard the aircraft carrier USS *George Washington* in 2008, and the hard grounding of the cruiser *Port Royal* in 2009. In each case—as well as in other instances of the mishandling of ships at sea—the doctrine of full accountability has been strongly enforced in the U.S. Navy, and will continue to be at the very heart of command at sea.

The Independence of the Commander

Traditionally, American commanding officers have been directed to accomplish missions without being told specifically *how* to do so. Occasionally they may be referred to doctrine or example about how their tasks might be performed or how they have been carried out in the past. The choice of action, however, remains theirs to make; it is required only that their methods intelligently support the objectives of command.

In recent years, however, this traditional independence has been modified in practice. The issue today is not too much liberality, but rather a growing tendency of high command to exercise control in great detail. There are several factors contributing to this trend. First, command in the present-day atmosphere of worldwide political unrest requires extraordinary sensitivity to an extremely complex web of global relationships. The post–Cold War world has complicated the missions undertaken by individual ships, submarines, and aircraft squadrons. Second, the ability of global media organizations to place the spotlight on naval operations has increased exponentially over the past few years—and will continue to do so. With network and cable news such as CNN flying overhead and the wire services constantly requesting and obtaining permission to visit U.S. Navy warships at sea, the latitude of the CO to act independently has been proscribed simply as a result of the unrelenting glare of publicity. Third, and most significantly, technological advances have given the entire chain of command the ability to track and direct virtually every aspect of naval operations at sea.

In this sense, technology has flattened the chain of command. The capabilities of our billion-dollar Aegis destroyers and cruisers illustrate this point more fully. A ballistic missile defense (BMD)–capable ship can simultaneously be involved at the tactical, operational, and strategic levels of warfare: tactically employed in a local antisurface, antisubmarine, or antiair warfare mission; operationally engaged in a theater missile defense mission; and strategically as part of a multi–time zone BMD fire control system providing national defense to our homeland. Along with these high-tech capabilities is the need to synchronize and coordinate their employment. Coordination requires connectivity at multiple levels of command, and it should come as no surprise that providing missile defense to cities and population centers will invite senior-level scrutiny. Likewise, an amphibious ship, engaged in humanitarian assistance and disaster response efforts at one moment and then rapidly shifting to duties as an afloat forward staging base (AFSB) for a joint task force elsewhere in a given theater, operates astride a confluence of tactical, operational, and strategic missions.

In hand with the increased capability that technology brings is a complementary capacity for assistance via "reach-back" mechanisms that leverage staff expertise and compiled data from across the globe. This can be tremendously powerful—but also overwhelming—if not managed properly. Notwithstanding all the "help" from outside sources, there is still an extraordinary level of responsibility on the shoulders of the captain. The CO will make the decision whether or not to fire in an individual engagement; when and how to tactically execute boardings at sea; when and how to undertake a medical evacuation—indeed, the time, method, and ultimate execution of a thousand discrete decisions remains the responsibility of the captain. In most cases, higher authority will respect the judgment of the captain at the scene, and there is little likelihood of that changing in the near future.

2 "YOUR COMMAND TOUR"

(Selection from chapter 18 of *The Professional Naval Officer*)

James A. Winnefeld Sr.

In **2006 Admiral Winnefeld wrote** *The Professional Naval Officer: A Course to Steer By,* which provides useful career advice to naval officers. While this book covers the entire officer career spectrum, the chapter dealing with first command serves as a kind of primer for the officer about to embark on her or his first command tour. Solid practical advice is illustrated by a number of examples gleaned from this impressive officer's own career.

"YOUR COMMAND TOUR"

(Selection from chapter 18 of *The Professional Naval Officer: A Course to Steer By*) by James A. Winnefeld Sr. (Naval Institute Press, 2006): 143–59.

> From the moment you, as the new skipper, step aboard you are on trial before your officers and men. Responsibility for the ship as well as for the men is yours.—Capt. Harley F. Cope

In this chapter I am talking principally about a sea command tour in the grade of commander. Some able few will get the plum of an earlier command (particularly surface warfare officers because there are more junior commands in that warfare community), but command in the grade of commander is your goal. For some it will be their only command. Major command in the grade of captain comes later and to relatively few. Just as battalion command is the key intermediate objective for Army and Marine officers in the grade of lieutenant colonel, command of a ship or air squadron is the goal for the unrestricted line Navy commander. This command is where all the threads of your professional voyage come together.

The path to such command was covered in my earlier book on naval officer performance and suggested in outline by the earlier chapters in this book. That path varies by warfare community. In this chapter you will not find a primer on how to be an outstanding commanding officer. There are books that specialize in the subject and an entire professional literature exists on the art and science of military command (such as *Command at Sea* by Stavridis and Mack). What you have read so far in this book foreshadows the particular challenge of command. You still must lead subordinates, you still must be professionally competent, and you still must ensure that your boss (e.g., commodore or air wing commander) gets all your help in meeting his or her mission.

In this chapter we focus on what a good solid command tour means in your overall career development and in preparing you for higher responsibilities. A command tour tests you in adversity and success, in managing and leading, in tactical decision making and seamanship or airmanship, and in understanding the Navy's business. You will find that the good things you previously took for granted are the result of hard work—by someone—and that your role is putting people, machinery, and good decision making together to make those good things happen. You will find yourself stretching to reach a higher level of performance because a large number of people are depending on you—your Sailors and your bosses. When you are done and finally turn over command to your relief, you will do so with a mixture of regret and relief—relief to be leaving behind the pressure to perform at a higher level than you would have thought possible before assuming command. You will find that future promotion and screening boards will be intensely interested in your command tour: what you did, how the command was employed, and how well your boss evaluated your performance. The competition continues. You will be measured with and against your brother and sister skippers, using an absolute standard of failure or success, and even against your predecessors as your reporting senior or selection board members recall their own days in an equivalent command.

Your detailer will also be keenly interested in how you are performing or have performed in command. Just being ordered to command indicates that you are on the first team. Performing well on that team means you are destined for more challenging jobs. You will find that as a skipper, or as a post-command officer, many people are sizing you up and assessing your future. Some commands insist on and deserve (two different things) post-command commanders for key staff jobs. One informed observer (see page 62 of the July 2003 issue of *Proceedings*: "All Detailing Is Retail," by CDR Clay Harris) has noted that good command performance at sea can outweigh almost all other factors when you are being asked for or considered for future assignment. A solid sea command tour can outweigh any lack of postgraduate education, service in important staff assignments or Washington duty, or even being less well-known by service reputation.

Why this myopic focus on command, and the performance that justifies such assignment, as the sine qua non of a naval career? The simple answer is because as a skipper there is no place to hide, no one else to blame, and few to help you—it all depends on your professional competence, your will, your courage, and your dedication to your mission. You may have a successful career and rise to the rank of commander but unless you have proved yourself in command, you have not confronted and passed the highest test the Navy uses as a yardstick. Good skippers take a quiet pride in the job—some even glory in it—and take their relief as a demotion. They enjoy the challenges, the excitement, the hands-on work of their profession. Most like their people—Sailors and officers—and work hard to make them better and proud of their job and command. And when it is all over most of them will deserve the title of shipmate and friend.

Many a successful mentorship has been the result of performing well for a skipper who respected your performance. The same goes as well for air wing commanders and commodores who particularly respect your performance in command. To successfully complete your command as a commander is to become a marked man or woman before screening and promotion boards and the people who make the Navy's personnel assignments.

Your Brother and Sister Commanding Officers

Your air wing commander, commodore, or admiral has called a commanding officers conference; there will be many such in your career. You look around the table and you see your contemporaries, all successful in their profession. They had to strive just as hard on the way up as you did to sit at this table. The fact of the matter is that they are your competitors, but only in the context of future promotion and screening boards. For now each of you is a member of a Nelsonian band of brothers. Your boss if he or she is a good one—and most are—will strive to create an atmosphere of working together smoothly in a common cause and just occasionally introducing a whiff of competition. But he or she is very careful not to overdo the latter.

A sea story. Once while I was in command I worked for a very ambitious flag officer, one who was feared, respected mainly for his warfare competence, and heartily disliked by his subordinates. In many cases his first response to sub-caliber performance was to have the offender relieved of duty. This flag officer seemed to delight in calling a conference and then needling some of his commanding officers as to why one of their colleagues always seemed to do a particular evolution better than the others did. When this needling was done in the context of a luncheon in the flag mess, the wry observation of most attending skippers was, "Not what—but who—was on the menu."

The result of this flag officer's penchant for fostering an all-out competition among his subordinates was to poison the wells of professional cooperation in his command. Skippers more closely guarded their secrets of success or failure where previously they were shared for the common good. The level of suspicion among skippers was raised and some became more afraid of being fired peremptorily than of performing well and selflessly. Relations of the skippers with the admiral's staff became strained and the channels of information flow clogged.

While you have no desire to be such a skipper or such a flag officer, there is a nugget of wisdom in this story to guide you in your conduct with your fellow skippers and your bosses. You have it in your power to set an example of cooperation and comradeship with your fellow skippers. It goes without saying that you must avoid "doing handstands" before them for the boss's benefit. Your peers will be quick to notice. By your demeanor and willingness to be a good teammate you will secure the respect of all. All this requires great sensitivity, care, and tact. It also requires a level of candor and humility particularly when you personally have so much at stake (e.g., your unit's reputation and your career).

My experience tells me that much can be accomplished by skippers working together and selflessly when out of earshot of the boss and his staff. This is where the seeds of cooperation and respect are sowed, and the resulting crop to be reaped is a more smoothly running machine when the boss enters the room. There may be some skippers in your group of the "dog-eat-dog" school and they will complicate matters until they can be won over as team players. But the effort is well worthwhile and you will find that you have gained both teammates and friends who will themselves ensure your reputation is enhanced. You should work the problem, not the boss. Your best fellow skippers will help you.

A trivial side benefit of such cooperative conduct is the look on your common boss's face when in a circumstance where he or she expects a problem, you skippers have already solved it. First there will be disappointment that he or she could not have an opportunity to demonstrate leadership or decision making ability. Then there will be a smile of relief and pride that "his" (or her) machine is working smoothly under good leadership. Department heads reading this take note; the same lesson can be applied anywhere in the chain of command.

Studying Your Boss

Of course you will do this throughout your career—not just to be a better officer in the job you now hold, but to give you the background and experience to discharge higher duties if you are called to do so. While serving as a junior officer or department head you were looking *inside* your command when you considered your boss. Now as a skipper you are looking *outside* your command and perhaps on to the Navy as a whole. You now have a larger window on the Navy's world and it is a priceless opportunity. Your boss is now holding a major command or perhaps is a flag officer. You will notice that many of the same skills you have acquired are also required of your boss, but there are now additional skills coming into play.

These skills include integrating the efforts of a large number of units similar to yours and possibly integrating efforts of a number of units with very dissimilar capabilities. They include devising ways to ensure information flows across commands, not just within commands, and that the boss is receiving timely and accurate information he or she needs to make effective decisions. You will also note that your boss is having to lead from a point somewhat removed from where problems are started. Most of these bosses will be keenly aware of command prerogatives (yours) on one hand and the need to maximize the output of the larger organization on the other. If your boss starts to meddle in your command's affairs, it may be that officer lacks confidence in himself or you. The latter should be of particular concern to you. Your first order of business is to conduct matters so that your boss is reassured that you are doing your job—and ever so subtly that you can do it better if your boss focuses on his or her own. Some admirals try to be the captain of the flagship. Flag captains get on by getting out ahead of their admiral. Don't let small things get between you and the boss. Fix them and thank the boss for his or her help in bringing the matter to your attention.

I know one outstanding flag officer who insisted that when he boarded his flagship that he be "bonged" (receive arrival honors) when his foot first hit the quarterdeck. To be bonged earlier, when his car hove into sight, or later when he was being greeted by the officer of the deck and staff watch officer, was unacceptable. Failure to observe this punctilio resulted in much needling of the flag captain who in turn drove his navigator (in charge of watch officers and the quarterdeck) to extreme measures to fix the problem—and fix it they did.

Afterward when asked informally about his insistence on this aspect of rendering honors, the admiral replied, "If they get that right, chances are they will get the rest of it right. The Navy starts with details done well and builds up to major missions done well." But there was an added payoff: the flagship from top to bottom knew the embarked admiral was paying attention and was holding their skipper (and them) to very high and exact standards of performance. A postscript: This flag officer and his battle group successfully completed a very arduous deployment and the former had good reason to sing the praises of his flagship and her skipper.

Command Responsibility and Prerogatives

Often when skippers are convinced they are receiving too many "rudder orders" (detailed instructions from on high and unnecessary for a well-run command) they will lament that the scope of action for today's skippers is much narrower than it used to be. They will cite instant communications and fast information flow among echelons as factors in robbing the commanding officer of time-honored prerogatives. Sometimes such high-level direction is necessary particularly when major political and strategic factors are at issue.

I remember as skipper of an amphibious ship evacuating refugees from Cyprus being told to come up on a high command net and to receive detailed orders directly from the National Military Command Center in Washington. Three command echelons above me were thereby wired out of the problem. It turned out that the nationalities of the refugees (some of whom were badly wounded or injured) were an important factor in selecting a safe haven port in that very troubled region for delivery ashore. But such instances are rare and in almost all cases justified. In my experience complaints about "rudder orders" as inhibiting the exercise of command are overblown—and sometimes involve an attempt by the skipper to be a player and a referee at the same time. As skipper you still have absolute responsibility, accountability, and authority. While modern communications and information systems put the boss at your elbow more than you like, he or she will be very hesitant to overrule you—and thereby accepting personal responsibility for the result in your command.

That is not to say there won't be nervous Nellies and second-guessers in your chain of command (mostly on the staffs), but you are in charge. Nervous staffs imply a nervous admiral somewhere. You need to consider such individuals as "part of the playing field" not an impediment to doing your duty. They will be long on advice and short on accountability.

Several decades ago, one CNO responded to the temptation to put his personal stamp on the way the Navy was run down to the deck-plate level. His fleet-wide messages included directives that many interpreted as telling commanding officers how to perform their duties. While there was a short-term payoff in personalizing leadership from the very top to the very bottom, a high price was paid in command accountability and engagement in the problems then at hand. More recent CNOs have had a phobia about putting out Navy-wide directives that in any way infringe on the prerogatives of the chain of command—meaning at its most basic level, you as commanding officer.

There is a nugget of wisdom in this discussion that applies to your own reach within your command as skipper. You will be sorely tempted to intervene in one of your departments—a temptation that is particularly acute if you have once been a department head in that field—and bring your expert knowledge to bear. When you experience that temptation ask yourself how you would like your boss to respond in a similar situation and proceed accordingly.

Looking Back

You will find that as you proceed up the career ladder you will often go back to your first experience as a commanding officer, reaching for the wisdom that will serve you well in dealing with the problem now at hand. I have a single piece of advice when you do that: Look at the mistakes you made (and probably weren't noticed at the time) and learn from them as well. Life is more than just leaping from one triumph to another; it also consists of adjusting your fire to reach the target. Among your mementos your first command at sea badge should be the most treasured.

3 "JOURNAL OF A FIRST COMMAND"

ADM James Stavridis, USN

In April 2008 *Proceedings* published this article, an excerpt from his then-forthcoming book, *Destroyer Captain* (Naval Institute Press, 2008). In it, Admiral Stavridis provides a personal glimpse into the world of a commanding officer of an *Arleigh Burke*–class destroyer. Although published years later, it is based upon his real-time entries into a personal journal that he kept while in command. Most striking in these reflections is the sense of awe and wonderment that complement the professional wisdom that shines through, leaving the reader with little surprise that this destroyer skipper was destined for greater things.

"JOURNAL OF A FIRST COMMAND"

By ADM James Stavridis, USN, U.S. Naval Institute *Proceedings* (April 2008): 64–69.

We sailed this morning for Haiti. What can you say about the first under way as a new commanding officer? I was nervous. All morning, I kept thinking ahead to the various commands that would move my beautiful, nine-thousand-ton destroyer off the pier. We were moored port side to Pier 25, and I mentally walked through the orders that would launch us toward Haiti—make up the tugs, single up all lines, take in all lines, all back on both tugs, all ahead one third, right full rudder—and all the countless permutations and possible combinations of wind and current and tide that might affect the under way.

Dodging a Bullet

Haiti looms, malignant and slightly nonsensical, just over the horizon. The seas have picked up, perhaps to sea state four, with a significant chop and over twenty knots of wind blowing, although it is clear and beautiful and we can see all the way to the dusty foothills of old Hispaniola.

The ship motors along apace. Today's crisis was a very near disaster. A major fuel oil spill inside the module of number three gas turbine generator. A moment to explain:

Our ship's electricity is generated by three large jet engines, which turn generators and power the ship. Today one of the generators suffered a fuel spill inside the module that encases it. The potential for catastrophe in such situations is very high, because if the stream of pressurized fuel had hit a sufficiently hot engine component, a major fire could have resulted.

At a minimum, such a fire would knock out about a third of the ship's electrical capacity and destroy the expensive engine.

This would necessitate pulling off station and steaming, with our figurative tail between our legs, into Puerto Rico for an engine repair.

At worst, should the fire have spread to the surrounding engine room, the ship itself could have been endangered by explosion and, at the darkest side of the equation, by many deaths and great damage to the ship. It has happened at sea, and not long ago, in a *Spruance*-class destroyer.

Fortunately, that was not the case today.

An alert watch stander in the space saw the stream of fuel coming out of the generator and punched the generator off the line before the fuel-air mixture could explode. We were helped by the fact that the generator itself was quite cold, having been off the line since midmorning. We spent the rest of the day cleaning and sorting out what had happened—the normal problem—people rushing to do a job had not completely bolted down a pressurized fuel connector line between the fuel filter and the rest of the generator.

The sound you hear is a bullet whizzing by all our heads on good ship *Barry*.

Like I told my engineer, "Sometimes you are lucky and sometimes you are good. Today we were lucky. From now on we need to be good."

Out and About

I feel better today, having spent much of the past twenty-four hours roaming the ship.

All captains are different. Some can govern effectively from the relative obscurity of an Olympian detachment. I think of a captain more as a servant than as a master, so I must know the needs of the crew. The best way to learn the needs of the crew is from their mouths to my ear, through conversation in the thousands of unlikely quiet (and not so quiet) corners that make up a U.S. Navy warship.

Thus, I am apt to be found in conversation in the forward engine room, the sonobuoy storage locker, or the mess decks rather than sitting at my desk doing paperwork. I am lucky in one way—paperwork is easy for me, especially at the moment with my superb second in command, Charlie Martoglio, who sends only photo-perfect documents to me. Thus, I can give each a quick review and sign with full confidence that we won't get ourselves in trouble.

That frees me up for my walkabouts, which occur two or three times a day, and always involve talking to at least forty or fifty crew members each day. I think I therefore have a good sense of what goes on, good and bad, below my decks.

Helping me are a network of people throughout the ship who I think are good barometers of crew morale and sensibility—the command master chief, Stan Brown, who moved his office to a small space next to the chow line so that he sees literally every crew member two or three times a day; the chief master at arms, the ship's cop, if you will, who ensures good order and discipline as well as the kind of good morale that comes from high standards and pride; the career counselor, who has a steady stream of individuals coming and going through his small office discussing the pros and cons of a Navy career in this turbulent era; the executive officer, of course, with whom I spend about an hour each day at various times covering the topics that ignite and decompress our small city at sea; and many, many others—from seaman to the ship's barber, they all have a story to tell, a data point to contribute, to the tapestry that is the USS *Barry*.

Plane Guard

The last twenty-four hours have been the hardest of this young command tour.

It began with twelve hours yesterday—from noon to gild' night—around the huge, dangerous aircraft carrier *George Washington*. There is a function that destroyers like mine perform for the carriers, called "plane guard." It is where I drive my relatively tiny nine-thousand-ton ship into a very tight station—about fifteen hundred yards—behind the monstrous one hundred-thousand-ton carrier. The slightest wrong turn by the carrier, and she will cut my ship in half.

Such a fate is not idle speculation. It has happened twice since the Second World War, most recently when the cruiser *Belknap* was hit and almost sunk by the carrier *Kennedy*.

The CO of the *Belknap* was court-martialed and disgraced. Interestingly, the son of that CO served as combat systems officer on my last ship and was a terrific ship handler—best I've ever seen. I suspect his dad was too; but when the carrier hit, he was down in the wardroom watching a movie. When I read about the incident, years ago as an ensign, I thought, "Well, I might not make the right decision as a CO, the great and perfect ship handling decision that would have saved the ship; but I will at least be in a position to make it—I'll be on the bridge whenever my ship is in plane guard around a carrier."

So, yesterday I chained myself to the bridge throughout the long afternoon—when there was enough light to see the carrier clearly—and through the still longer night, when it was black and overcast and raining hard and all I could make out—only fifteen hundred yards ahead—was the dim light of the landing pattern lights on the carrier. We turned and sped up and slowed down and played in the Shadow of the enormous ship—like a dog playing under an elephant that might at any moment decide to sit down on you and end the game rather abruptly. And we came through all right, . . . I was only really nervous once, when the carrier swung around me and faced straight at me, and I could see its bow light a few thousand yards away, seemingly innocuous except when you think of the enormous tons and tons and tons of massive ship hurtling along behind that single white light.

We cleared from plane guard about midnight. For the next five hours, I tried to sleep but couldn't. Tossing and turning, full of coffee and the danger high, I waited, called over and over again by my watch standers, for the lightless dawn. At dawn, the seas were higher than I've seen them in the mid-Atlantic this time of year. The reason? The poetically named "North Wall" effect. When a cold high pressure center hits the warm air of the Gulf Stream—once in a while this time of year—it creates sudden massive seas. Up to twenty-five feet of tossing and turning green water, vision obscured by blowing foam and scud, fully overcast sky without a discernible horizon—that is the bleak end. We haven't hit that—yet.

But this morning was the worst I've seen in long time. The ship rode well. This class is designed to be a good "seakeeper," a wonderful maritime expression that means it rides smoothly despite the effects of the sea.

When the message came in predicting the North Wall effect, we had a brief moment of euphoria, hoping we would be ordered into port. No such luck, however. Instead, we were ordered north into a storm haven at sea, an imaginary box on the ocean's surface, where we patrol hopefully, awaiting the return of good weather.

And that is where dawn found me, the dawn weak and pallid, bleak and gray. And I, tired, drawn, looking forty-five instead of thirty-eight, a bristly beard and two days without a shower, with five ships within a mile of me, a dozen radios chattering different directions, and a complex shiphandling exercise to complete ahead.

By 1300 it was all over. We had spun the ship through its paces, turning and wheeling and exchanging stations with the other ships in the line, stretching me and the executive officer thin, but finally getting it done.

Sub Hunting

It has been a demanding week of antisubmarine warfare, that greatest of all artistic feats of war—the hunting, finding, and killing of submarines.

Submarines are like steel sharks—quiet, silent, and deadly. They are designed to hunt and kill. Occasionally, it becomes necessary to find and destroy them—to keep open sea lanes of communication, to sweep an area and make it safe for allied shipping. Destroying a submarine, I think, is the hardest task in naval warfare. The submarine must be found within the roiling ocean.

The nuclear ones travel deep—over a thousand feet—and fast: they are as quick as any ship. Many advantages are theirs—stealth, counter detection range, speed over most ships, sensors. Yet, surface ships have advantages too. They carry torpedoes, both ship launched and rocket thrown, with ranges out to eight miles. Better yet, they carry aircraft that can harry the submarine for hundreds of miles, much like a coon hound can eventually bring down a convict. And they have reasonably capable sensors for picking out a submarine in the depths—sonars with ranges over a hundred miles passively and twenty-five miles actively.

So, our task—that of my ship and half a dozen others under the command of a senior captain—is to find two submarines and simulate killing them. We spend five days hunting up and down the east coast of the United States, searching, localizing, and attacking. At the end of the week, I think we have done well—my ship's tally is fourteen confirmed attacks, and we have held contact on the submarine consistently.

Yet, the submarines have gotten in their shots as well, and they have launched a fair number at our ships.

In a real war? Who knows? I think our surface force gave roughly as good as we got—which is a tribute to the small force of only two U.S. submarines. Of course, this is antisubmarine warfare against U.S. submariners, the best in the business.

Against third-world submarines and submariners, I am confident we could carry the field with an even greater degree of certainty, assuming our attack included aviation assets and, better yet, our own U.S. submarines. But there is simply no question that submarines are deadly weapons of war and have an asymmetric advantage in ocean combat.

Looking at Eternity

The ammo is aboard, some of it bright and shiny, some old and corroded, all of it swung aboard on big pallets run across the churning water between the two ships as we cut through the sea. It is interesting to realize that some of the gun rounds were manufactured before I was born, back in the early 1950s. Old ammo—like old soldiers, I guess—never dies. It just gets slung from ship to ship as the deployment dates come around.

After the ammo load, our next tasking was to pick up one of the heavy amphibious ships and escort it to the shore for a mission of recovering pilots downed inland. We provided shotgun services. The ship was an LPD [amphibious transport dock], a large, heavy gray hull commanded by a senior captain. I tried to stay out of its way, which wasn't easy because our two ships were twisting and turning in the rising seas all morning. The situation wasn't helped by the sudden appearance of a dense fog, which made the LPD vanish from sight, even though it was only a thousand yards away.

When the fog hit, I backed the *Barry* out to about four thousand yards and tried to keep track of the amphib on the radar. A frustrating morning, and I nearly, for the first time in years, lost my temper with one of the ensigns who had the conn. The ensign just didn't keep full situational awareness of the danger inherent in the weather and proximity to a big, badly handled ship. I kept it cool, but I had a better and more experienced conning officer take the conn. Inside, I was seething with the ensign's lack of initiative and competence—and he a Naval Academy graduate to boot.

After a trying four hours close to the shore on top of the amphib, I was stunned to receive a call to proceed to the flagship, the distant carrier *George Washington*, for briefings on a "special mission" for the *Barry*. The seas were rising high by this time, the weather closing in, and I was in no mood to fly to the aircraft carrier. But the admiral called and off I went.

I hated to hand the ship over to the XO and the wardroom.

It was, of course, the first time the *Barry* had ever been under way without me—or without a captain, for that matter, as I'm sure my predecessor never left the ship while it was under way. The barometer had dropped significantly, and I told them to run down the seas, heading for a rendezvous with the oiler. Then I strapped into the small Lamps MK III helicopter—my courtesy ride from the USS *Doyle*—and headed off to the carrier.

As the small helo lifted off and headed into the buffeting wind, I found myself looking at the thunderstorm clouds and thinking, I am looking at something. What is it, I asked myself? A moment's reflection, and I felt the cares of the day and the frustrations of the moment drain out of me, along with anxiety for the meeting ahead. I realized that in the face of those big black clouds, which form and reform endlessly over the uncaring sea, that all of this will pass along in its due course, leaving very little in its wake. As Joseph Conrad, the greatest sea writer of the nineteenth century, said of this sort of sight, it is "the magic monotony of existence between sky and water." In the end, I am looking at eternity.

In twenty-six minutes, the helo touched down gently and smoothly on the massive flagship's stable and placid deck—for the carrier, ten times the size of the *Barry*, responds not at all to the wind or the rising seas.

Special Mission

On the carrier, I met very briefly with the rear admiral commanding our battle group. He had just received word he was to have a second star, and seemed happy and a bit distracted, as though something important—more important than talking to a commander—was about to happen. That benign distraction, I thought, was the natural reaction of about 99 percent of all admirals to the presence of anyone junior to them. It was something I consciously tried to avoid in the *Barry*, but in fairness, I was, of course, much closer to the people who worked for me—who numbered only 340—than the admiral, who had ten thousand and more working for him.

He told me to get with the SEALs for the special mission briefing, said we were doing a great job—something he tells everyone—and dismissed me.

I wandered into the flag mess and found the SEALs, a lieutenant commander, a lieutenant, and a lieutenant junior grade. All were right out of the movies—attractive, sandyhaired surfer looking guys. Their plan was pretty loose and basically consisted of the *Barry* using her stealth qualities to sneak into the beach and bring out a SEAL platoon, which had been doing some kind of special operation ashore.

We discussed communications, water depth, night vision devices, signals, procedures. I briefed them back. They seemed surprised I could remember what they just told me. And in a few moments we were done.

I took my charts and scribbled notes back to the *Barry*—after a quick chat with my immediate boss, the commodore—and was safely back in my own wardroom, on the badly pitching deck, within the hour.

Night Extraction

The SEAL pickup went flawlessly.

As I sat on the bridge wing, watching the sun go down—slowly—at 1900, I really understood the meaning of the special forces motto: We own the night. All I wanted was darkness, when my nine-thousand-ton destroyer would simply melt into quiet blackness, radar systems and sonars silent, and become a small blip on a dully watched coastal radar, lit only by the dim bulbs of a "fishing boat."

Finally, the sun set, and we motored slowly the final twenty-five miles in the dark at only seven knots, wondering if the SEALs would make the rendezvous. They were scheduled for a window from 2200 to 0100, and I suspected we wouldn't see them until well after midnight. Yet we had no sooner slowed to two knots at the rendezvous point than I heard the excited call of the OOD (officer of the deck) for me to come to the bridge.

I saw them first with the low-light night vision devices mounted on the bridge wings—two winking, distant lights, tiny and small on the roiling sea surface, closing the ship.

A silenced motor of some kind, and suddenly they were alongside the ship, zipping under the bow, and I turned sharply to starboard and made a lee from the wind.

They clambered aboard, huge and burly in the dark night, four-day beards, loaded with gear. We fed them a hot meal, tossed their gear in a corner of the helo hanger, turned into the wind, and their helicopter arrived and swept them back to the carrier.

And we were left a hundred miles in enemy waters, our SEAL mission complete. I turned the ship away from land and motored gently into the black night.

Unbelievably Old, So Young

We have six midshipmen aboard from six different colleges. All seem like impressive young men in different ways, although two of them have told me they have no interest in the surface Navy and instead are interested in the Supply Corps and intelligence, respectively.

I have always been confused as to why on earth you would sign up for the Navy if you want to do anything besides drive ships or submarines. If you want to fly, it might make more sense to join the Air Force, although the challenge of landing on the rolling deck of an aircraft carrier has obvious appeal to the very daring. Yet, I suppose the basic allure of going to sea has an appeal, even for those who aren't directly in the ship line of business, and of course we're lucky to have good pilots, supply officers, and intelligence officers who support what we do at sea so well.

Still, I spend time with all six, coaching them on the bridge, on shiphandling, on leadership, on life at sea. I feel unbelievably old at thirty-nine talking to midshipmen in their early twenties. They are so utterly unformed.

And I look at my face in the mirror, the faint lines around my eyes, grown from looking into too many dawns at sea after long night watches. My thinning hair, the hard cheekbones, the thin, frequently tired face. It is the mask of command staring back at me in the mirror, I suppose.

God, the midshipmen are so young. Too young to be at sea.

4 "COMMAND AT SEA—THE ULTIMATE SPECIALTY"

CAPT William J. Holland Jr., USN

Later achieving flag rank and well-known for his writings, then-captain Holland penned this thought-provoking treatise on command at sea in December 1976.

Emphasizing the role of command as the "quintessence of the naval career," he observes that "when old admirals gather, they swap stories about their commands at sea—not their battles in the Pentagon."

In an apt metaphor, this veteran submarine commander contends that "fine dinners are not prepared by merely competent cooks. As the skills of a fine chef, nurtured in years of careful experience, are evident to the palate of a gourmet, so is the skill of a fine commanding officer evident to those professionally able men who serve over and under him."

Captain Holland also makes the interesting observation that when a commanding officer receives an ALNAV (all Navy) message directing command attention to some particular topic, it is an indication that "every other echelon in the Navy has failed, and it is now up to him to execute the task."

Some of this thought-provoking article was devoted to recommended changes in procedures and policies in the Washington domain that were worthy of consideration at the time but are no longer relevant, and those portions have been largely deleted. What remains here is cogent advice that commanders and command-aspirants will find valuable and, in some cases, provocative and challenging.

"COMMAND AT SEA—THE ULTIMATE SPECIALTY"

By CAPT William J. Holland Jr., USN, U.S. Naval Institute *Proceedings* (December 1976): 18–23.

Command at sea is the quintessence of the naval career. When old admirals gather, they swap stories about their commands at sea—not their battles in the Pentagon. Unfortunately, all too often an "old-timer" can be heard to remark, "I wouldn't want a command today; it's not fun anymore." This is followed by laments about hard work, stiff inspections, excessive administrative burdens, inadequate personnel, oversupervision, and so on. That the "old-timer" may be a lieutenant speaking to ensigns marks a drastic misperception in the working levels of the Navy.

The denigration of command at sea is not wholly a problem for which the Bureau of Personnel or the Navy hierarchy is at fault. While the Navy as an institution must select and assign the commanding officer, arrange the external management around him to support, encourage, and enhance his efforts and status, and—where necessary, remove him—the commanding officer builds most of his own self-esteem and position of accomplishment. A commanding officer often fails to transmit to juniors his uniqueness of position and the importance of his task.

It is generally recognized that—viewed from above—the whole ship's personality and performance are reflected in the commanding officer. Not so well realized by all ships' captains is that they are "the Navy" to all below them. Each commanding officer epitomizes, in a way unique to his profession, all the theory, liturgy, and ability with which his juniors will endow the entire organization.

Looking up from below, there should be no "they." The buck will always stop in the commanding officer's cabin.

In this regard, the commanding officer must look to himself as the first person who may be denigrating his position. He should not be looking outward for solutions to problems but inward to himself and to his own ship's company. Somehow, officers still arrive at command with a notion that someone else will make the machinery work or provide the "trained" replacements to accomplish the maintenance and operation of the physical plant assigned to their custody. But the commanding officer is that person to whom all the rest of the Navy, above and below, looks to do this task. He has to acknowledge that while there are some experts at particular specialties, there is no one on board who knows more than he can find out. Moreover, the training of every man in the ship is the captain's responsibility—a responsibility he can share but not delegate. To do this successfully, he must participate actively and personally in that training. As he does so, he will discover a wonderful fact: he is training himself.

Commanding officers must manage their ships. The Navy still lives from crisis to crisis, but if the crisis manages the ship instead of vice versa, the captain is reacting and not managing. As the seat of many diverse pressures, the commanding officer must resolve the conflicts, serve as a buffer, and sort the priorities for the whole command. This is the crux of his involvement in the management of his ship. It is his decision, based on his knowledge of his people, his resources, and framed in his own judgment. No one has enough time or resources at any level to make this judgment easy or clear. But in the final analysis, it is the individual commanding officers who are the ultimate arbiters of what is good for their ships.

While lamenting sudden changes and short-fused requirements, most commanding officers do not appreciate how much control they have over their ships' schedules and operations and how total is their internal control. The commanding officer can easily forecast what he needs within his ship and predict what operations and upkeep are going to be needed in the future. In respect to his own ship, he can be much more accurate than the fleet scheduler. By planning further ahead than the scheduling authority, then informing the scheduling officer of the ship's needs and wants, the commanding officer can influence the actual scheduling to a greater degree than he realizes. There have to be some compromises, and there will always be the necessity for a ship to perform operations not necessarily to the commanding officer's liking. But, amazingly, most schedulers try to accomplish the commanding officer's desires, if they know them. Recognition of this effort by the scheduling authority comes only if the commanding officer becomes involved with forecasting the long-term needs of his ship and the fleet.

In regard to type training and independent exercises, the commanding officer should be the ultimate planner. He not only must plan but also execute within his own ship the plans he has made. To take a ship to sea on exercises without a detailed plan is to lay the ship open to inactivity, ineffective training, and boredom. The ship's company much prefers activity to idleness and will respond to working hard at sea. Such planning and execution need to go into evolutions during transits as well. The captain who ensures that every minute of the ship's time at sea is profitably occupied will find he not only has a more efficient ship but that he needs less time at sea to keep her that way.

The involvement of the commanding officer in the details of his ship directly correlates to his control over them. Upper management intervention is required in almost every evolution. This intervention can take the form of standard organization manuals, bills, and procedures which greatly assist managers by removing questions in areas of small import, thus leaving them free to work on areas of larger decisions and problems. In other circumstances, it may mean the captain personally assists a quartermaster plotting a fix: thereby training the quartermaster how something should be done and training himself on what can realistically be expected. This is not robbery of initiative but a participation by the commanding officer in the actual work of his command. The captain, his senior officers, and experienced petty officers have to demonstrate, teach, monitor, and participate at every step to train the less knowledgeable and less mature personnel.

If the ship is out of control or inefficient, it is because the commanding officer lets her be so. Vigorous training, active planning, consistency of policy, and his involvement in all phases of training and maintenance will get her under control fast. This control is so total and complete as to defy description; it is not duplicated in any other situation. Not even the President of the United States has so complete a control. "Poor Ike," said Harry Truman, "he'll come in here and say 'Do this' and 'Do that' and he'll think it will really get done." Command at sea offers a unique opportunity not only to practice total management control but to exercise the most direct and dynamic leadership possible in the officer's entire career.

Several fallacies inhibit commanding officers from the total involvement implicit in the preceding prescription. There is a desire for independence from control and accountability which is wistfully compared to that of a yesteryear which did not exist. Before departing to open Japan a hundred years ago, Commodore Matthew C. Perry was given his orders by the President of the United States in person. While careful instruction from such high authority has not been routine, the concept of total accountability and careful adherence to significant instructions has always been the hallmark of a commanding officer acting in the best interest of his country.

There exists, too, the idea of command as a sinecure: a long-dreamed-of and well-fabled "home at three," a grand magisterium, lord of countless vassals who would do all the detailed work while the commanding officer makes grand decisions based on concisely presented, clear-cut alternatives. On the contrary, command means hard work, buffeted by the directives and capriciousness of superiors and a vast array of pressures in which enthusiasm for the task and sincere interest in the command's mission and the people who serve with, not for, the commanding officer are the bulwarks of success.

In such an environment, the captain can simplify his task by keeping the mission of his command in mind. This does not mean that the ship should be ready to go anywhere to do anything at any time. In the long haul this is destructive to both material and personnel readiness. It does mean the training of the junior officers and senior petty officers to solve sailors' problems, whether they be getting to school or fixing the fire and flushing pump. When problems are not solved, sailors look to their chain of command for reasons why. To them the chain of command stops where it ceases to be visible at the commanding officer. He thus needs to establish an environment where the problems get solved not simply by issuing structured orders. He must create a framework of working relationships which includes a positive approach, an atmosphere of approval, personal attention, interest, and involvement. In such situations there always will be some problems—perhaps many—which cannot be solved to everyone's satisfaction, but the ship's company will know that it is doing its part, as is the captain.

The rewards for all this are not easy to identify. There is no extra money, but the commanding officer does have better quarters than his subordinates. He can come to work after quarters if he so chooses. He is addressed by a truly majestic title. However small these and other similar items may seem, the psychic income can be overwhelming. The captain knows in his own mind that when the AlNav is received directing "Command attention to . . . ," every other echelon in the Navy has failed, and it is now up to him to execute the task. The total commitment of a crew and ship performing a useful mission provides the captain with an unmatched sense of fulfillment since it is his personality, effort, and ability which bring these men and this material to fruitful purpose.

[. . .]

Fine dinners are not prepared by merely competent cooks. As the skills of a fine chef, nurtured in years of careful experience, are evident to the palate of a gourmet, so is the skill of a fine commanding officer evident to those professionally able men who serve over and under him. And as the chef matures in the kitchen, not in the drawing room, so must the service mature its commanders at sea, not in Washington. Most of the day-to-day problems facing the Navy are solved at the unit level, not at graduate schools or by high-level staffs. Discussing this issue in terms of the Army's crisis of leadership several years ago, Major Lewis Higenbotham prescribed the solution, ". . . the best people must go to troop duty." Those officers who aspire to command should be encouraged and assisted at every preparatory step of their careers. They should be nurtured within the limits of their career assignments, while at the same time carefully culled to eliminate all but the finest performers. This means repeated tours at sea in similar ship types with shore duty in billets directly relating to their warfare specialties.

Not every officer of the Navy is fitted for, deserves, or wants command at sea. To recognize this does not involve the proliferation of more badges or insignia or job codes. Such recognition does involve the identification of potential commanding officers early and their detailing to repeated sea tours within their warfare Specialties as part of the restructuring of institutional policies needed to enhance the status of and attract our finest officers to command at sea. Lengthening command tours, establishing effective, acknowledged chains of command senior to the commanding officer and a recognition that the shore establishment is less vital than the operating forces are other components of an unemotional approach toward improving the internal cohesiveness and efficiency of the operating forces.

The view of Admiral Gorshkov that "the commanding officer is the leading figure of the Navy" is unfortunately not echoed in our day-to-day affairs. More often "the commanding officer's attention is directed to . . ."—a harsh imperative not always reserved for important or even substantive matters. A change in attitudes both for individuals and as institutional policy is important if we are to retain the commanding officer expertise Admiral Holloway claims as one of our greatest assets. Command at sea must be viewed as the most important part of any career. The performance of officers in such command is more important than any amount of subspecialty designation or postgraduate education in valuable but peripheral fields. Every assignment and all training before achievement of command status should be pointed toward its proper fulfillment.

We, the Navy, must return to recognition of our ultimate specialty—command at sea.

5 "COMMAND PRIMER"

Maj E. J. Markham Jr., USMC

Shifting from command at sea, this article—written by a Korean War veteran while subsequently attached to Headquarters, U.S. Marine Corps—provides a "grunt's" view of command, offering practical advice on what to do *and* what *not* to do. However, much of what is proffered is applicable to all commanders, no matter what the color of their uniform.

"COMMAND PRIMER"

By Maj E. J. Markham Jr., USMC, U.S. Naval Institute *Proceedings* (May 1961): 125–29.

Command is the ultimate honor the Corps can bestow. It is a privilege, not a right. It is complete and absolute—an end in itself. It brings with it a degree of responsibility that is unmatched in any other profession. It is the "moment of truth" in the career of any officer.

We who are Marines have cause to be proud of our past commanders. Their record speaks for itself. It is equally important that we be able to point to our newer commanders with the same kind of pride, for the future of the Corps rests squarely on their shoulders. To this end, the Corps must place increasing emphasis on the selection and development of its commanders. All officers must devote more study to the subject of command as an integrated process.

> *—What are the prerequisites to command?*
> *—What pitfalls confront the new commander?*
> *—How do you command?*

These are questions that perplex any officer assuming command for the first time. These are questions that new officers must be trained to answer for themselves. This article does not presume to answer these questions completely. It does provide a framework within which, hopefully, they can be more readily resolved.

What are the prerequisites to command? Command requires intelligence, knowledge, integrity, experience, maturity, and respect for your fellow man. The personal attributes that could be listed are almost endless. Most important, however, it demands a balanced intellect and a sense of proportion.

The very title of "General" attests to this need. The commander must be a generalist. He needs a broad outlook. He requires versatility to cope with changing situations and new environments. He must have the capacity to lead a variety of different type units. The one characteristic he must have above all else is the ability to distinguish between the important and the unimportant. Until he develops this, no man is qualified to command.

What pitfalls confront the new commander? The pitfalls confronting a new commander are many. Two, however, must be regarded as paramount. The first concerns the ability to define objectives; the second, the capacity to render selfless service.

The officer who cannot define objectives will fail as a commander. The officer who cannot render selfless service . . . who cannot place his unit before his personal ambition . . . will also fail. What is worse, the units such men command will have little chance for success.

This can be illustrated by showing what happens to officers who succumb to these pitfalls. The examples which follow are presented for this purpose. It is noted that the types of officers sketched are few and far between. That they exist, to a greater or lesser degree than depicted, serves as warning to us all. Take a good look at ten who will never make the grade as commanders:

The Ambitious Administrator

This officer magnifies the importance of administration. He regards it as an end in itself, and insists that everything be in writing. His unit is a paper mill specializing in the manufacture of orders, directives, and SOPs. When he has an SOP for everything, he writes an SOP for SOPs and starts all over again. His outfit usually looks good on paper, but it can rarely cut the mustard in the field.

The Good Egg

The Good Egg is everybody's best friend and his own worst enemy. He strives to please everyone. His men will be happy whether they like it or not. Nothing is too good for them; and that's exactly what he gives them. In trying to please everyone, he pleases no one. He avoids unpleasant decisions and lacks the heart to take disciplinary action. He keeps putting off such matters until he confuses and demoralizes his entire unit.

The "I've Got It Made if I Don't Foul Up" Type

This officer is essentially *negative* in character. He is somewhat surprised that his career has taken him as far as it has, and is more concerned with protecting what he's got than he is with advancing further.

Command is, in his eyes, an unfortunate interlude between more plush assignments. He can survive it so long as he makes no horrible mistakes. With this in mind he elects to run his unit in a defensive manner. He keeps himself in defilade so that it will be difficult for his superiors to get a good "shot" at him, and refuses to stick his neck out. He does nothing unless he has to. When he is forced to act he insists on a reference to cover himself.

The Caustic Critic

Officer's Detail has the uncanny knack of always assigning this officer to the most fouled up outfit in the Corps. This is a secret he keeps from no one.

He scuttles morale in his unit the moment he assumes command by openly criticizing the unit and his predecessor. Never content with letting a sleeping dog lie, he continues to drop constant reminders of this throughout his tour. One cannot help but feel that he criticizes solely to camouflage his own sense of inadequacy.

The Politician

This commander devotes half of his time to figuring out which way the wind is blowing and the rest to selling himself to his superiors.

His decisions are never based on what is good for his unit but rather on what is good for himself. He is quick to seize the opportunity to talk to his boss, but only tells him what he thinks the "old man" wants to hear. He is noted for his lack of originality and adeptness for taking credit for things he hasn't done.

He usually poses no puzzle to his troops. They are quick to recognize him for what he is. Their typical reaction is to avoid him, take it easy, and pray for his early relief.

The Wild Bull

The Wild Bull's philosophy is simple: *People are no darn good.* He doesn't like them, and he doesn't trust them.

His is a reign of terror. He gets things done by cursing, shouting, threatening, and bullying. He rules as an absolute dictator. He runs roughshod over his officers and men, convinced that courts martial, letters of reprimand, and unsatisfactory fitness reports will solve all problems. The irony of his predicament is to see an officer charged with preserving a free society discard all the principles of that society to carry out his duties.

The One Man Show

Early in his career this officer received an unfavorable fitness report because one of his subordinates "goofed." He has vowed that this will never happen again. His solution is obvious. He can't count on his subordinates, so he does everything himself. He works day and night, seven days a week. The harder he works the farther he gets behind. He and his unit commence to crumble at the same time. He usually leaves by way of the dispensary. Diagnosis: ulcers or nervous tension.

The Procrastinator

This officer has but one fault; he can't make up his mind. He always needs more time to think things over. Routine problems take on major proportions. Liberty chits must be submitted a week in advance; leave papers a month. Reports lie around until higher headquarters demand them. His troops often sit idly by doing nothing, then work nights and weekends to catch up. All because the thought of making a mistake so horrifies him that he just won't or can't make a decision.

The Born Leader

The Born Leader has compassion for others who labor at command. He has never had to bother. He is a born leader whose natural instincts and intuition permit him to solve all problems in a moment. Let other officers study and gather facts, he'll have none of it. He can always rely on his hunches to extricate him from any dilemma. This type is quick to blame others when things go wrong. He often becomes embittered when his seniors pass him over and promote other officers with far less natural ability.

The Petty Perfectionist

This officer becomes so absorbed in detail he lets the big problems go right by. He'll spend two weeks supervising the construction of a new paint locker and approve an annual budget in five minutes. If you clocked him you would find that he devotes 90 percent of his time to minor problems and 10 percent to major ones. His reasoning is quite simple; the little things he understands, the big things escape him.

How Do You Command? We have discussed some of the wrong ways. What is *the right way?* This is a difficult question to answer, for each officer must command in accordance with his chosen ways of leadership.

It is extremely important, however, that all officers recognize that command is a responsibility that cannot be assumed casually. It requires considerable advance thought and planning. The new commander will find that developing a commander's check list will assist him in formulating his policies and procedures. An example of such a check list is presented on the following pages. While this list does not solve all problems it will enable the new commander to get a more balanced perspective of his duties.

The Commander's Check List
1. Study
Study your future unit. Learn everything you can about its mission, organization, operations and procedures. Learn its strengths and its weaknesses. More important, get out and talk to the men who make it tick. Get a look at the unit from their point of view.

2. Define Objectives
As you study your command, define what its objectives must be. List these objectives in order of importance. Don't be surprised if some of them conflict with one another. They always do. If this confuses you, think how much more it confuses the troops. Decide how much time and emphasis you will place on each objective, and how you will handle those that conflict.

3. Set Standards
When you know your unit's potential, set the standards of performance you expect it to meet. Set standards for the entire command, its subordinate units, and for every officer and man in it. Once you set these standards, insist that they be met. Never tolerate substandard performance.

4. Plan Progress

Don't wait for the future to take care of itself. It never does. Plan the progress you want your command to make. Decide how far you will move toward each of your objectives within set periods of time. Move your unit toward these objectives at a steady and regular pace. Don't run hot and cold. Don't move in spurts. Be particularly careful of radical and sweeping changes at the start. A unit is often like a fast moving car; if you turn too sharply or too fast, you may lose control.

5. Lay Your Career on the Line

Once you assume command, you graduate from penny ante poker. This game is for table stakes, and your stake is your career. Accept this challenge by laying your career on the line. Take your finger off your number, heave your "bluebook" in the nearest G.I. can and TURN TO!

Recognize that your outfit always comes before your career. Base every decision you make on what is good for the unit instead of what is good for yourself. Anyone who accepts command with a lesser sense of responsibility does not deserve it.

6. Communicate

The minute you assume command, establish communications with your officers and men. Maintain these communications throughout your tour.

Keep your men informed of your objectives, standards and plans. Let them know what you expect of them; and what they can expect from you.

This process of communication is perhaps your most vital function. Lack of information, or misinformation, is a basic cause of all leadership failures. Informed Marines don't make mistakes. When they know what must be done and why, they will do a good job.

To this end, keep your channels of communication open. Don't just publish an order and expect it to be carried out. Posting a piece of paper on a bulletin board guarantees nothing. Teach your officers and NCOs how to get your "message" across to the troops in words that will be understood.

Be particularly wary that your officers and NCOs don't set up communication blocks within your chain of command where they edit and censor facts, passing on to you only what they think you want to hear. Give these men the word! Keeping bad news from you only hurts the unit.

7. Command

If you assume command, you must COMMAND! Your sole function is to give your men purpose and direction. Provide them with the decisions they need to carry out their duties.

Don't put off. Don't hesitate. Don't wait to see what will happen in two months. Call them as you see them! If a decision is required to keep your outfit running smoothly, make it as quickly as possible on the basis of the best facts that are available. Don't be afraid of making a mistake. The greatest single crime you can commit against your troops is to do nothing.

8. Organize

The whole is greater than the sum of its parts! This is the essence of organization.

Build your unit to get the greatest productivity out of the assets you have available.

Use your Table of Organization as a guide, but don't be confined by it. You'll never have the men listed in it, so learn to get by on less. Don't build an empire. Anyone can run an outfit with 25 percent more men. It takes leadership to run it with 25 percent less.

Be careful that garrison duty doesn't change the basic organization of your unit. Your command is designed for combat. Don't permit its organization to become so modified by stateside frills that combat will come as a surprise. Keep this need for combat organization uppermost in the minds of your men at all times.

9. Work

There is no easy way to command. At its best, command is a difficult and demanding job. It requires work, work, and more work! Work at it continuously. You cannot afford to let up for a minute.

10. Reserve Judgment

Judge your unit on its merits. Don't criticize the man you relieve, or the unit as it is when you take over. This serves no purpose. Your men will accept such criticism as criticism of themselves. It gives them a sense of insecurity. They will suspect your motives and support you reluctantly. Reserve judgment until you have set your standards and given the unit an opportunity to meet them.

11. Respect Your Men

Respect is a two-way street. If you want your men to respect you, respect them. Preserve their individual dignity and privacy. Back them up in everything they do. See to it that your officers and NCOs adopt these same attitudes.

Do not tolerate prejudice in any shape or form. Prejudice is a civilian luxury. Men who exist solely to fight together as a team cannot afford it.

12. Use Your Subordinates

Don't try to run the organization by yourself. Use your subordinates. Delegate all the authority to them that they can possibly handle. Then train them to handle more.

Force them to accept responsibility!

Force them to utilize their initiative!

Force them to think!

Challenge them to expand the limitations they place upon themselves!

Never allow them to become smug, satisfied or complacent!

13. Use Authority with Restraint

Use your authority with restraint; always hold some in reserve. The CO who has issued his "last warning" has little to fall back on.

Do not hesitate to take disciplinary action when it is warranted; but don't use such action to threaten and bully people into getting things done. If you always have to fall back on your rank to get things done, you don't deserve the rank you have. Motivate your men so that they will carry out your orders because they recognize their need and importance, not because you outrank them.

14. Innovate

Don't be a book soldier. Don't put up with red tape. Don't let tradition tie your hands behind your back.

Be an innovator!

The book is at best a guide. The mediocre commander uses it as a crutch. The enterprising officer has the ingenuity to change it.

Always keep an open mind. Be receptive to change. Be willing to experiment with and test new ideas. When you do find a better way of doing things, don't keep it a secret. Share it with all.

15. Build Pride

You can't issue pride to your troops. You must build it. Do this by permitting your men to retain their self-respect, and by building up their sense of responsibility and accomplishment.

16. Give Credit

Give credit where credit is due. A pat on the back never hurt anyone and it costs you nothing.

Be wary of taking personal credit for anything your unit does. You don't rate it. You serve only to focus the efforts of your men. They do the work.

17. Give Your Boss the Word

Give your boss the word. Keep him informed of what is going on in your unit, both good and bad. Don't just tell him what you think he wants to know. Tell him all he needs to know to run his outfit regardless of how it reflects on your ability.

Never hesitate to ask him for his advice. This is not a sign of weakness on your part. It's what he's getting paid for. He can't help you unless he knows your problem.

18. Stay Out from Behind That Desk

Don't be a slave to paper work. Turn this over to your exec and get out from behind your desk. You get a much different perspective of your unit when you're out in the field with your troops than you do from the after end of your office.

19. Be Yourself

Know yourself and be yourself. Don't try to be a "carbon copy" of another commander. Methods that work for one officer may not work for you. Recognize your own limitations and use those leadership techniques that are best suited to your personality.

20. Retain Your Sense of Humor

Don't be afraid to laugh at yourself or your efforts. If you can't, you've had it. The troops know that you have to keep your distance, but there has never been a law against a commanding officer acting like a human being.

It is recognized that the comments on command appearing in this article may not meet with the approval of all officers. If, however, they cause a single commander to take a new look at his unit, to become more aware of his responsibilities, or to devote more time to the study of command, they will have served their purpose.

6 "THE PRACTICAL APPLICATION OF THE PRINCIPLES OF HIGH COMMAND"

CAPT Harris Laning, USN

Reminding us that *Proceedings* has been around for a very long time, this article that appeared in December 1922 is a bit dated in places, but it offers some sound advice and is thought provoking, providing a point of departure at the very least. The author distinguishes between high and low command, promotes a number of essential characteristics, and concludes that the principles of high command are "embodied" in a "trinity—self preparation, planning, and execution."

"THE PRACTICAL APPLICATION OF THE PRINCIPLES OF HIGH COMMAND"

By CAPT Harris Laning, USN, U.S. Naval Institute *Proceedings* (December 1922): 2041–62.

During recent years military and naval officers the world over have been devoting more and more of their attention to the principles governing the exercise of command, and many are the books and papers that have been published on the subject. While not a few of the writings are invaluable to those who exercise command, nevertheless practically all of them treat the subject from a theoretical rather than from a practical point of view. However essential theory may be to the development of any art or science, it is not always necessary that he who practices the art be an expert in the *theories* upon which it is based, nor does it follow that one who is a good theorist will for that reason be good in practice. Hence many of the writings on command are not of great help to the practical man in doing the actual work, for having filled his mind with theories, and probably sound theories, he is often at a loss as to how to apply them to his everyday work. It is the belief of the author of this paper that the "practice" of command, like the "practice" of navigation, engineering, or any other activity, can be so described that one can perform it with fair success even though not a great expert in the *theory* of it, and it is the intent of this paper to outline what appears to be a practical method for insuring successful *high command* in naval forces.

So far as the naval service is concerned *command* is of two distinct types. One type, which we may call low command, is more generally concerned with controlling men as individuals and in leading them while carrying out the wishes of a superior; the other, which we may call *high* command, concerns itself with controlling the unified efforts of groups of men through directing the commanders of the groups. Between the two types there is a great, though not always recognized difference. In the former the commander is always a follower who merely carries out the ideas of another, while in the latter the commander is always a leader who *creates the ideas* as well as directs the carrying out of them. It does not follow that a man who is excellent for low command will by virtue of that fact excel in high command, for it is one thing to lead on a way devised and directed by someone else and quite another to devise, direct, and lead the way for all others.

In the Navy the line of demarkation between high command and low command usually lies somewhere *above* the grade of captain. Up to the time he leaves the captains' grade, an officer's work is generally confined to that of low command. Starting with the grade of ensign, each duty of low command naturally prepares one for the next higher duty in that command, and an officer profiting by experience can pass along the line through the grade of captain without finding it absolutely necessary to give much study and thought to the principles of low command. As a subordinate he has no great difficulty in carrying out the duties assigned him, probably having an excellent division, department, or ship. He may or may not have analyzed the principles of low command and applied them to his work, though if he has he is undoubtedly a more efficient officer. Up to the time he leaves the grade of captain, and possibly for some time after, the average intelligent, energetic and conscientious officer exercises command passing well, and it is frequently assumed that when he has done so he has thereby become fitted for the high command that comes with further promotion. Such assumption is utterly unsound and is dangerous in the extreme. While it is practically certain that an officer who fails in low command will hardly excel in high command, it does not follow that mere success in low command proves one's ability for high command. On the contrary there are many men who, under the leadership of efficient *high* command, can obtain excellent results while commanding a ship, a division of ships, or other subordinate unit, but who have not certain altogether different essentials required for high command. It is the purpose of this paper to discuss those essentials and to then point out how they may be developed and applied.

Before starting a discussion of the essentials, attributes, or principles peculiar to high command, it would be well if we could digress long enough to consider those of low command, for there can be no doubt that as far as they go the principles of low command apply also to high command. However, it is not the purpose of this paper to deal with such elementary principles. It is assumed that all officers are more or less well qualified for exercising low command and that all are continuously preparing for the higher task when it comes. Hence for the moment we are not so much concerned with what we *have been* or *now are* as we are concerned with what we *must be and do* if we are to succeed in high command. Most of us are approaching a point in command where we may cease to be the followers of leaders to become the leader of followers, which change is very great and which we must be ready for when it comes. What must one be, what must one do to succeed in this new form of command?

Before we can deduce an answer to our query it is necessary that we have a full understanding as to just what is meant by command. In the *Century Dictionary, command,* as held by persons, is defined as "the right to order, control, or dispose of" and carries with it "the right to be obeyed or to compel obedience." This definition covers the meaning of the word as it is generally understood, but analyzing the definition we cannot but be impressed with the fact that although it states much as to the *rights* possessed by one who commands, it says nothing at all as to the responsibility and duties of a person when he possesses those rights. That command carries with it responsibility and duties as well as rights is evident, but just as they are omitted from the definition they are not always given the consideration they should receive even by those who reach positions of high command. Thoroughly informed of the *rights* that go with command, not all understand or appreciate what such rights impose, yet it is what they impose that is the very essence of success in high command.

It is not difficult to *order, control,* and *dispose of* when one has the power to *compel* obedience, but to do those things in the way to get the best results is an altogether different matter. That they must be done in the one best way in military or naval forces is evident, for unless they are, not only will the forces themselves pay it. From this it must be apparent that that which actually constitutes command, viz., "rights," is possibly the least important part of it while that to which no reference is made in the definition, i.e., the responsibility and duties of command, is the very thing on which all success in command rests.

It is much to be regretted that the definition quoted above is so generally accepted, both in the service and out of it, as the full meaning of the word *command.* The idea that a Naval Academy education, a commission, and an officer's uniform, if coupled with a long life in the service in positions of low command, are all that is required for high command is not entirely confined to civilians. All too many naval officers have that idea and seem to think that those things are practically sufficient in themselves to make a man function perfectly in the art of high command. As a matter of fact those things are the most primary and minor elements of high command. Having them, the officer is merely at the starting point. Whether or not he functions properly thereafter depends upon himself.

It has been said that truly great commanders, like Napoleon and Nelson, are born, not made, and there can be no doubt that some men have a natural bent for high command that others have not. However even the greatest in high command, born to it though they may have been, reached their pinnacle only because of their preparation for their tasks. And the same processes must be gone through with by every successful commander. Not one has or will become great through mere intuition and environment, and hence no matter on whom the mantle of high command may fall, it remains for him to fit himself for the work. Were it possible to make the mantle fall only on those who have the natural bent for it, filling positions of high command would be much simplified, for such men would instinctively prepare themselves. As yet, however, we have no means of ascertaining which officers have that bent, hence all who approach the zone of high command must prepare themselves for it even though not fore-ordained to succeed in it. Each one must so educate himself that he will know what to do and how to do it, and then, having that knowledge, must develop the qualities both in himself and his command, that will enable him to make his forces do the things he wants done, in the way he has decided to do them.

From the above it would appear that there are three fundamentals for success in high command:—*First*, knowledge of exactly what is to be accomplished; *Second*, ability to lay out the certain way to accomplish it with the forces at one's disposal; and *Third*, skill in directing and leading the forces commanded so they will do the thing to be accomplished in the way decided on to do it. If he who holds a position of high command develops these three fundamentals, *knowledge, planning, execution*, his success is certain. Therefore let us see what he must do to develop them.

Up to the time he starts preparing himself for high command, an officer is not compelled to familiarize himself with anything but the immediate tool with which he works, such as the gun, the turret, the engine, the shop, the plant, the ship, or, at most, a small group of ships working as a unit. He comes to know rather definitely, or at least should know if the work of his higher commander has been thorough, just what each tool he has been associated with must accomplish in any situation. Also he has been indoctrinated in the way the tools should be utilized to accomplish it. His work has therefore been rather simple and his responsibility comparatively small. But on taking up the work of high command all this changes. He no longer thinks in small units or operates one or more small units, but must operate many units of many kinds, in a wide range of activities, and solely to attain the end in view in a way determined by himself. While his knowledge of details and the previous training he has had are undoubtedly essential in the new position, by themselves they help him not at all in it. Unless he knows how to combine all the parts of his command into one great machine, and can make that machine do his bidding, he does not function as a high commander. True he may wear the uniform, occupy the position, and assert his "rights;" also he may put up the semblance of a machine; but when the test comes the machine will fail and in its failure bring disaster to itself and to the country that owns it.

Before one can develop a machine for making successful war he must know what such war is. Hence the *first* step toward high command is a study of war—what causes it, what will constitute a decision, and what principles of strategy and tactics should be followed to gain decisions. Such study of war can never end as long as an officer may be called on to exercise high command, for only by keeping up to date in all things pertaining to war can the officer hope to keep himself ready to wage it successfully. However, when he has progressed to a certain point in his study of the conduct of war, the officer must learn to apply the principles in planning and carrying out successful operations pertaining to war. This is the *second* step in preparation for high command and in this phase the officer must get actual practice through war games. By such practice he learns to correctly estimate situations and reach sound decisions as to the courses of action he should take to win out in any situation, and if such practice is continued he finally becomes expert in drawing up plans that will bring victory in war.

The two steps of preparation just now so briefly outlined can be partly made by taking the courses provided by the War College, but owing to the limitations of the correspondence course, and to the shortness of the regular course, neither step will be complete unless supplemented by constant work along similar lines. Both before and after the War College courses the officer must study and practice war operations, constantly endeavoring to broaden his knowledge and make himself more expert in the conduct of war. But no matter how far he continues such work it is after all only a preliminary to high command. However great one's knowledge of war may be or how remarkable his ability to plan successful operations, he cannot *win* unless he makes his machine carry out his plans. So we now come to the final and most important fundamental of command, *execution*, the practical and successful application of theoretical preparation.

Just as there are many officers who believe that command begins and practically ends with the "rights" of the commander, so there are others who think that it ends when one knows the principles of warfare, and is more or less expert in *planning* war operations. While the latter idea is possibly not so utterly wrong as the former it is still so far wrong that he who believes it is but little better fitted for high command than he who believes the former. Knowledge of war and ability to plan war operations will not by themselves gain decisions in war and this must never be forgotten. Sound plans based on even full knowledge of war bring favorable decisions *only* when they are properly executed. This being so it behooves us to go deeply into the matter of *execution*.

What must a high commander do to insure that the forces he commands will carry out his plans successfully? Operating on a sound plan, forces *organized* and *indoctrinated* for their task, well *disciplined* through proper *training* in *team work*, *loyal* and of *high morale* will always win the decision if it is humanly possible to do so in the existing situation. Therefore the answer to our question as to what the commander must do to make his forces succeed seems to lie in (1) Organization, (2) Indoctrination, (3) Discipline, (4) Training, (5) Team Work, (6) Morale, and (7) Loyalty. Let us discuss each of these until we clearly see not only its relation to the execution of plans but also how we may develop it in the forces we command.

Until he is actually given the position, the work an officer does in connection with high command is expended entirely on himself. But when he enters high command and starts to execute, the officer deals with others, many others, who know neither his ideas nor his methods, who are not organized or trained to meet the requirements of *his* plans, and who have little to bind them to him. Yet all of these he must take unto and make a part of himself and his machine.

If he is to succeed he can no longer rest content with doing only what he is told to do or what routine requires him to do, but on the contrary must act, act vigorously, and along the right lines deduced by himself. Having no one above to drive him, he must initiate, push, and drive on his own volition until his machine is assembled and in every way ready to fight, for until it is assembled and ready the machine is useless for his purposes, and the high commander has failed in the duty his country implicitly trusts him to perform.

The first step in developing a war machine is to organize it properly to do the work it will be expected to do in war. Such organization is much less difficult to bring about than is generally supposed provided that *efficiency for the task* is made the criterion. Unfortunately, and all too often, those in high command sometimes let other things than fighting efficiency dictate the organization of their forces, and as a result they frequently wind up with commands that can do almost anything but the one thing they are wanted for, fighting. We have had this situation even in our own Navy and will continue to have it whenever organization is based on anything but the fighting factor. Therefore on coming to a position of high command, the first thing an officer has to do is to make estimates of the situation, ascertain who the probable enemy or enemies are, determine the fighting his command may be called on to do in case of war with them, and then decide on how he will carry on the fight and on his *task organization* to fight that way. This *task organization* for war, derived from those estimates, is the organization a commander should use for his forces, not just during war but during peace as well.

Editor's Note

A portion of this article has been deleted here because it refers to an old system of naval organization that is no longer relevant.

The great obstacle to efficient organization in any Navy is the generally prevalent idea that there should be or can be a difference between its peace organization and its war organization. One might as well expect a team organized for baseball to win a football championship as to expect a Navy organized for peace conditions to win in war. If a team thinks and lives baseball it can't do much in football, and a Navy that thinks and lives for peace can never win wars. Yet to a certain extent that is the way in our Navy today, and anyone who comes to a place of high command in it, if he hopes to succeed, must bend every energy toward remedying that defect at least in the part of it he comes to command.

Just what causes a Navy or any part of it to continue in an organization based solely on types of ships and peace administration is hard to say, but it would appear to be because those in high command in such a Navy think in terms of peace rather than in terms of fighting. Possibly they know war and can plan war operations, but if so, they fail in the final test of high command for they do not prepare their forces to *execute*. We who are now preparing for high command must not follow that example for even though those who set it may not pay a penalty it does not follow that we also will fail to pay it. Therefore let us resolve that when high command comes to us we will immediately organize our forces for the work they should be ready to perform. It may not be easy to do; it may possibly make peace administration more difficult; and it may even meet with the opposition of some who do not or will not think in fighting terms, yet for all that we must do it for otherwise some of us are doomed to defeat, and our country to disaster.

Having organized his forces for war, a high commander must next indoctrinate them with his ideas and plans for waging it, for no matter how perfectly *organized* forces may be they cannot function as a fighting team unless each part knows exactly what is expected of it. Without indoctrination a huge Navy even when properly organized, is very like an "All American" football team, in which each position is filled by *naming* an exceptionally strong and able player, but which has never been assembled as a team and taught a way to play together. If the eleven men named, as the "All American" football team this year were suddenly brought together and started in a game of football against a reasonably strong team, no matter how excellent and how strong the individual players are it would still have but little chance of winning. It would be exactly the same way with a war team. Unless the parts filling the various positions on the war team know exactly what is expected of them in every situation, and know exactly how to do it, they cannot win. Teaching them what to do and how to do it is known as "indoctrination."

Were it possible to carry on war by means of fixed rules, the indoctrination of a Navy, a fleet, or a force, by its commander might not be absolutely necessary for with such rules one could turn to them and get an approximate idea of his part in any particular operation. However there are no such rules and, for naval forces, there never can be any. No two commanders will ever do exactly the same thing in any of the infinite variety of situations that arise in war and so whenever a high command is taken over by a new commander, even though the old commander has indoctrinated the command with *his* ways, it is still essential that the new commander at once start his indoctrination. And it is especially necessary that he do so in our Navy, for, possibly excepting the battleship force, no part of it is as yet fully organized for its war tasks or indoctrinated with *anyone's* ideas or plans for war. Not fully ready to wage war in accordance with anyone's ideas it is much less ready to wage it in accordance with the ideas of a new commander. Under any circumstance, but especially under circumstances such as still exist to a large extent in our Navy, a new commander must not delay his work of indoctrination. Like organization it is vital.

Indoctrinating the command is one of the longest and hardest parts of the work of a high commander, yet the indoctrination must be thorough. Just how to proceed with it is often confusing and it is to be regretted that many officers, even graduates of the War College, do not understand how it is to be attained. Some seem to think that indoctrination should come from or through the War College, but that can never be for the War College makes no pretense of laying down fixed rules for conducting war. Even after taking the course one officer will have one way of doing a thing and another an entirely different way, both ways being sound and in accordance with the best principles of warfare. The way to be followed by any command is, of course, the way of its commander, hence when indoctrination is attempted it must be done to accord with that commander's plans. If subordinates in the force have had the War College course the commander's work is much simplified, but whether they have had the course or not they must still be indoctrinated. How, then, may we go about doing it?

Subordinates are said to be indoctrinated when they have become so imbued with their commander's ideas that, given a task by the commander, they will execute the task in practically the same way he would if performing it himself. Therefore the commander must cause his ideas to be absorbed by his subordinates until they actually think and act as he would or as he would want them to. Naturally this cannot come to pass if the commander stays away from his subordinates or keeps his ideas, plans, and methods to himself, so he does just the contrary. He constantly holds conferences with his officers regarding the operation and handling of the forces; he assumes war situations and explains how he wants the command to act in them; he assumes other situations, issues orders for the operations they demand, and causes the orders to be carried out by the subordinates in accordance with ideas he has enunciated to them; he trains his subordinates in order reading and order writing; he teaches them to estimate situations as they apply to their forces, to come to decisions as he would, and then to operate their forces in accordance with those decisions; he makes them realize that in their work all are striving to the same end, and he teaches them co-operation and co-ordination of effort. All these, and many other things, he must do, and he does them not with one officer at a time but with all the heads of the main subdivisions of his force gathered at conferences or games. Doing these things with those immediately under him, he requires them in turn to indoctrinate their subordinates, and so on down the line through the whole chain of command until the whole force works as a unit, united in thought, united in action.

As things are in modern navies, it often happens that neither the high commander nor his subordinates are familiar with all the uses or are well versed in the capabilities and limitations of the various forces and the new types with which they are working. Even in our own case it is often impossible for the "High Commander" to proceed rapidly with his work of indoctrination because neither he nor anyone else knows exactly how to handle the new and not fully developed weapons. Even after all his preparation and training he must to a very large extent develop his plans and ideas after working with his forces to learn what they can do. Such procedure has been found necessary in our destroyer forces where the development of destroyer tactics and such indoctrination as is possible in a faulty "type organization" are going on hand in hand. However, in spite of the handicap, indoctrination is going on in those forces just as it should be in every force and in every part of the Navy. But it will never go on *everywhere* until each officer holding a position of high command rises to the occasion and carries out his duty rather than just rest content with exercising his "rights." Not the least important part of that duty is the indoctrination of his command.

The next step beyond indoctrination in preparing a command for its task is to make it "well disciplined." Let us get clearly in our minds what is meant by a well disciplined force. Specifically discipline is "training to act in accordance with rules," and forces are disciplined only when they have been so trained that they will always *act* in accordance with the wishes of their commander. In bringing forces to the state where they will always act in the way desired, the training sometimes becomes severe and corrective of faults by punishment, and, because of this, to many officers discipline has come to be so associated with chastisement and punishment that it is thought of only in connection with them. Officers having this idea seem to think that by chastising or punishing subordinates for anything and everything they thereby develop discipline in their command as well as a well disciplined force. That idea is not only entirely erroneous but possibly does more to reduce efficiency than any other one thing. Through forcing men not to do anything at all because they fear punishment if they do anything, it tends to defeat the very thing the high commander wants to accomplish. Discipline is never punishment. On the contrary it is a state or condition brought about not by punishment but by careful painstaking teaching and training on the part of the commander, by which a force becomes able to act in accordance with rules which are the commander's wishes as enunciated and taught by himself. While punishment for failure to so act is sometimes necessary it otherwise has nothing to do with disciplining forces. When constant punishment has to be resorted to it is *prima facie* evidence that the command has not been *trained to act* properly, and the fault lies not with the subordinates but with the commander himself. Not until the commander has taught and instructed his command in his ways, and has trained them *to act* in accordance with them, can he possibly have a well-disciplined command.

A high commander must not try to hide his own neglect of duty by punishing his subordinates for not doing the things he has never told them he wants done. He may sometimes, and especially in peace time, evade paying the penalty for his shortcoming by using the power of his position to throw the blame on the helpless subordinate but he will never have a *trained* command. Punishment must be meted out when deserved but it should go to the one who deserves it, and unless he has truly trained his forces to his ways this will frequently be the high commander himself. As a matter of fact in a force trained to act in accordance with its commander's wishes, punishments are few because they are unnecessary. Training, not punishment, makes a disciplined force, and if the officer reaching high command will but bear this in mind and carry out what it implies he will have not only a force that will act *in accordance with his wishes* but one that will do so under *any* condition however impossible that condition may seem.

Since training and not punishment makes a well disciplined force, how may a commander go about such training? We have seen the steps he takes to organize and indoctrinate his force but training goes far beyond that. True, during their indoctrination the higher officers get something akin to training but it is at best only on the game board and is theoretical rather than practical. What the commander now wants is to put theory into practice in exactly the way it will be done in actual war. Obviously to do that is impossible and the nearest approach to it lies in operations that are largely sham. But in sham operations it is not possible to cover every detail of actual war in one grand maneuver, hence it is necessary to take up the various phases part by part and carry out each in a way as nearly like actual war as possible. *Movements,* either strategical or tactical, can be practiced in "fleet maneuvers"; hitting with guns, torpedoes, bombs, etc., can be practiced through actually firing them at targets under conditions similar to those of battle; and other phases can be practiced each in its own way. And so after he has indoctrinated his force a commander must lay out a schedule of practical exercises, by which each and every part of his force gets actual practice at sea in everything it has to do in carrying out the plans for fighting as deduced by the commander. While we can never at one time hope to practice a force as a whole in all the details of its war operations, we can, by careful planning and taking the phases part by part, give the entire forte and every part of it a tremendous amount of practice at sea, and sufficiently like war, to fulfil our requirements. Hence as soon as the commander has given his force sufficient indoctrination to make it know what he wants to do and his general plan for doing it, he must plan and carry out a system of actual practice that leaves no portion of his force untrained or overlooked. Fleet maneuvers covering each phase of the plan, target practice in every form of firing the force will be called on to use in battle, speed trials, economy in steaming, self-upkeep, communication, and every other detail can be *practiced*, and must be practiced over and over, carefully, systematically, and thoroughly until the force not only knows exactly what the commander wants done but *can do it* with precision, certainty, efficiency, and each part in co-ordination with all the rest. For this actual training the high commander alone is responsible, and until he has carried it through his command will never be disciplined or become a fighting team.

In the treatment of our subject up to this point little has been said of the teamwork required in a great fighting force, although in a way teamwork must be considered in every step the high commander takes. His plans for fighting must be based on it, his organization laid out to enable him to put it into effect, his indoctrination such as to make the theory of it known to his forces, and his training work practice his forces in it. In all that an efficient high commander does, *teamwork* exercises a dominating influence, and yet strange to say the principle of teamwork seems to have been lost sight of in recent years by many high naval commanders.

It is possible that the failure of the British fleet to win an immediately decisive victory at Jutland was due to its poor teamwork; in our own Navy if the various elements of the fleet have fully developed teamwork either in themselves or between each other it is not in evidence. Neither in battle, nor in the phases of a campaign that precede it, can any naval force hope to gain success unless its parts are ready and trained to make a tremendous and *co-ordinated* effort, and hence an officer coming to a position of high command, and especially to such a position in our Navy, must devote great attention to *teamwork*. It is not sufficient to merely base plans in it, to organize forces for it and indoctrinate them in it. Having done all those things and having practiced each part of his force in its own particular task, the high commander must then train the parts as a *whole* in simulated war maneuvers. When he has done that, but not before, his command will be a *fighting team* and naturally no commander worthy of the name can ever rest content until his is a fighting team in fact as well as in theory.

A force organized to carry out its commander's plan, indoctrinated as to the plan and the way of executing it, and trained until it can actually carry the plan through in a perfectly executed coordinated effort has gone far in its way to being ready for its great task. Even then, however, it is not sufficiently ready and should a commander stop his work at that point his force will be far from being all it can and should be. Organization, indoctrination, and training, essential though they are, will not by themselves make a force always victorious. Back of those things there must be a greater quality, a *will to win*, and that quality must be so developed that the force will refuse to accept anything but victory. The quality in a force that gives it such a will to win that nothing less than victory will be accepted is known as morale, and it is so vital that unless a command has it to a superlative degree it not only may be defeated but probably *will be*.

Napoleon said "In war the moral is to the physical as three to one," and it is probable that if he erred at all he placed the moral factor too low. Certain it is that material things such as numbers, equipment, and perfection of operation can never bring victory to a force, unless that force is dominated by a will to win that victory. In spite of this self evident truth the training of forces is frequently focused on giving them the ability to fight while the *will to fight*, which is the far more important element, has been left to look out for itself, and this in face of experience, which shows that even with less actual effort the moral factor can be developed just as surely and just as highly as can the physical. Since the physical factor, no matter how highly developed, is practically useless for war purposes unless glorified by the moral factor, it follows that a commander must develop that moral factor to the utmost. The question for us then is how he may do so.

When a commander attempts to develop the quality known as morale he is confronted with something very different from the other phases of his task.

Whereas organization, indoctrination, training, and teamwork are definite things that require definite action to bring about, morale—the will to win—is a mental attitude, a particular mental attitude, that is so indefinite as to be almost intangible. What goes to make up the particular mental attitude that will not accept defeat under any circumstances that no matter what the suffering or loss may be still drives on to victory? What may a commander do to develop it?

Morale, for all purposes of war, is a state of faith; it is belief in an ability to see *anything* through to a successful conclusion; it is a measure of men's confidence in their cause, in their leaders, and in themselves. If this be true, we begin to have something definite to work on, for to develop morale it is only necessary to develop that confidence until it is absolute. And a system for that development can be devised by any able commander provided he himself has the measure of confidence he desires to inspire in his subordinates. Much of the work he can do himself and some of it no one can do for him, but a great deal of it can be done by a special organization put in the force for that particular purpose, provided the commander makes himself the *soul* of that organization.

It is impossible to lay out briefly the special organization necessary to develop morale in a force or to explain in a few words how such an organization goes about its task. However, it is unnecessary to do so for in certain books, like Colonel Munson's *The Management of Men*, both an organization and a system for the development of morale are so well explained that any high commander can perfect his own from them. Naturally the high commander should not delay starting the work along that line, but when he has done so he must remember that he still has other things to do to develop morale, and that these other things are *things no one can do for him*. Always his own example must show his confidence; always he must energize the system with the fire of his own faith; and always he must lead. While through his own efforts and those of his morale organization his forces may develop great confidence in their cause and in themselves, he must never forget that these are but two legs of the tripod that makes morale. The third leg of the tripod is the troops' confidence in their leader, and the structure will fall just as surely from the failure of this leg as from the failure of any other. Hence unless a commander can inspire confidence in himself as a leader he will never have a successful fighting force.

The confidence of a force in its leader is based primarily on the strong personality of the leader himself, and this personality includes ability, devotion, and justice. A truly great leader has little difficulty impressing his ability and devotion on his subordinates. During the organization, indoctrination, and training of the force they have ample opportunity to weigh both, and they will weigh them for exactly what each is worth. Any failure of a high commander to carry out his duty along some such lines as have been discussed in this paper cannot but be known to his force, and though by other ways he may keep their love, their honor, and even their respect, during peace time, when put to the crucial test in war, they are bound to question both his ability and his devotion. When subordinates do that, the will to win in the sense meant in this paper cannot exist. However, even though by his work he clearly impresses both his ability and devotion on his subordinates, a commander who is lacking in justice to them can hardly hope to exact their loyal support when facing trying conditions. Only justice begets loyalty and unless held by the extreme of loyalty men cannot and will not make the supreme effort or the supreme sacrifice called for in war.

Though loyalty is really only one of the many elements that taken together bring high morale, it has such far-reaching effect on morale that it deserves some attention, and especially so since all too often those holding positions of high command do not always understand its principles or apply them to themselves. While in the sense ordinarily used loyalty is devotion to a superior and therefore works upward from the bottom, in the military sense it works both ways and to have its maximum effect there must be loyalty down as well as up. This fact is often overlooked, and we not infrequently see a commander exacting *all* from those under him and giving them little or nothing in return. In fighting forces one-sided loyalty spells failure, for certainly no commander can expect from his subordinates anything more than he himself gives to them. The commander who fails to support his subordinates when they are faithfully trying to carry out his wishes cannot long count on their maximum support. The commander who in order to avoid punishment for his sins of omission or commission, throws blame on subordinates, has no right to expect, much less demand, devotion to himself. Yet time on time we see these obvious truths violated and find men who should be leading their subordinates to higher standards actually taking a low standard of action in their dealings with subordinates. How different it is for the commander who has the moral, courage to stand by and with his subordinates in their hour of need! When his own hour comes they will stand by him to a man and no effort or sacrifice will be too great for them to make when he asks it. Therefore in our preparation for high command and when we come to high command let us not forget that the loyalty of our subordinates to us and all we do will be measured in kind and amount by our own loyalty to them.

There is no better way for a commander to show his loyalty to his subordinates than by having faith in them to carry out any task he assigns. It is to warrant such faith that commanders go to such great lengths to indoctrinate and train their commands, yet it often happens that even after they have done so they nullify their work either by taking charge of a subordinate's task or by including in orders detailed instructions for carrying it out. Showing, as it does, a lack of faith, such action is fatal to results and if persisted in not only reacts in the subordinate's loyalty to his commander, but also tends to destroy his initiative, the very thing on which a commander must rely when not in personal contact with the subordinate. When a subordinate knows his commander depends on him to carry through successfully his part in the general plan, in the way that seems best to him as the man on the spot, he will spare neither energy nor resources in doing so as long as there is life in him. This is exactly the spirit and will to win that the commander wants and must cultivate; but it never comes to a force whose commander tries to do anyone's work but his own. For this reason, if for no other, high commanders must leave all details of execution to their subordinates. Nevertheless there is another and quite as important reason for doing so.

Whenever a high commander usurps the province of a subordinate he does more than kill initiative and destroy morale, he puts himself in a position in which he cannot but neglect his own great task. From what has gone before it is evident that in attending to his own important duties a high commander has quite all the work any man can do and that if he undertakes the work of another he can do so only at the expense of the time he needs for his own. Furthermore, in doing it he sacrifices the *whole force* to a part, and even the part becomes worse off than it otherwise would be because it is trained solely to operate alone. We see an instance of this when a Commander-in-Chief takes personal charge of say his battleship force, and personally supervises all it does while giving little or no attention to the rest of the fleet. Because that task keeps him very busy he may feel he is doing all he can do and his full duty. On the contrary he is doing nothing that he should do and is actually *neglecting* his duty. No matter how perfect the co-ordination of battleships may become between themselves it will serve no purpose in war unless the battleships *as a group* co-ordinate with those of the other parts of the *battle fleet.* Even a perfectly trained *battle fleet* will be of little value in war if it cannot co-ordinate its efforts with those of the other forces that have to lead it to battle. This being true it becomes nothing short of fatal when a Commander-in-Chief concentrates his energies on only one part of his force, for he stands not only to get nothing from his fleet as a team, but also to get the absolute minimum from the part he concentrates on.

In the same way that a Commander-in-Chief often fails through usurping the work that belongs to subordinates so will any other high commander fail who does likewise. Yet over and over we find high commanders doing that very thing. They swamp themselves in details belonging to subordinates, and because they overwork themselves in doing so they imagine they are making progress even though they never give a thought to their own great task. Success in high command is never measured by the *quantity* of work done by the commander but only by the work he does on his own particular task, and high commanders should not delude themselves on that point. To do so is absolute proof of incompetency and unfitness for the task. If a high commander cannot from his mission deduce his own task he certainly is not fitted for command. Neither is he fitted for it unless he sticks to that task, and to no other. In these two statements we have the very foundations of all success in high command—knowing one's own business and attending to it. When the high commander does that he does all, but the trouble is that many high commanders do not do it. Those who aspire to such positions should avoid the pitfall, but if they do it will be by their own efforts for there is no one else to point them fair.

What one must be and what one must do to succeed in high command is now before us. Even from this brief discussion it must be evident that he on whom the mantle of high command may fall has a responsibility and a duty he cannot evade without willfully exposing himself, his command, and his country to disaster. While those in position of low command always have over them a higher commander who is competent to judge, and who does judge and pass on their work, the high commander has no such superior and if he so elects he can often leave undone those things he should do without himself paying any penalty for it. During war, should he then be in command, his country of course will judge him by the results he gets. But war may not come during his time in command, so even though the evil of his way lives after him he may not be held responsible for it. Ordinarily during times of peace the sole judge of a high commander's work is his own conscience, and if he chooses to salve that it is probable that no power superior to him will either question or doubt anything he does or does not do. During such times, though he has utterly failed to prepare his force for war, it is even possible a high commander may be considered a successful one for at that time, at least outside the Navy, no one knows or seems to care about the Navy's readiness to fight. But can we as naval officers neglect our duty simply because of that? Are any of us so deficient in moral obligation and sense of duty that we are willing to turn over to a successor a command which if war comes might bring odium on him and disaster to the country? Let us hope not; but at the same time let us not forget that our own Navy is not today either a fully organized or highly trained fighting team. Were the way to make it a fighting team obscure, were there any doubt as to exactly what course a high commander should take to make it one, there might be some excuse for our not making it ready and keeping it so. But with the way so clear there certainly cannot be. Knowing that way, an officer worthy of the uniform he wears and of the trust his country has placed in him cannot and will not spare either himself or his efforts in following it.

Truly the principles of high command are embodied in the trinity—self preparation, planning, and execution—each of which follows the other in turn and none of which is of value without the others. Of these the first two concern themselves only with the high commander, but the last concerns itself with the entire command and is the measure of all that command does. No matter how well the commander may prepare himself, no matter how expert he may become in planning, those things go for naught unless he *organizes* his command to carry out his plan, *indoctrinates* it with the plan and method of carrying it out, *trains* it so it will act in coordinated effort in accordance with the indoctrination, and finally develops in it the "*fighting spirit*" and the "*will to win.*" These are the things the high commander can do and must do. And they are the things he will do if he too has the *fighting* spirit and the "will to win."

7 "ASSUMPTION OF RESPONSIBILITY—ESSENCE OF COMMAND"

CAPT W. P. Mack, USN

In January 1961 *Proceedings* published a particularly worthwhile discussion of the role of responsibility in naval command by then-captain William P. Mack while he was serving as naval aide to the Secretary of the Navy. By the time he retired as a vice admiral in 1975 after thirty-seven years of service, he had held numerous commands at sea and ashore, including the U.S. Seventh Fleet and a memorably successful tour as superintendent of the U.S. Naval Academy. His credentials for the subject at hand are exemplified by his coauthoring of the fourth and fifth editions of the Naval Institute's *Command at Sea*, among many other books and articles.

In this acclaimed article, Mack contends that "it is the duty of every officer who aspires to be a successful commander to make himself proficient in the recognition, assumption, and discharge of responsibility, both toward his superiors and toward his subordinates." He further urges the aspiring officer to "meet his responsibility eagerly and enthusiastically, to seek it out, and having found it, to live with it easily, fearlessly, and intimately."

"ASSUMPTION OF RESPONSIBILITY— ESSENCE OF COMMAND"

By CAPT W. P. Mack, USN, U.S. Naval Institute *Proceedings* (January 1961): 61–67.

In 1950 the American-owned Isbrandtsen Steamship Line was engaged in trading along the China Coast and in entering certain Chinese Communist-held ports. The Chinese Nationalist Navy was attempting to prevent entry by any ship into Chinese Communist Ports. This situation was under general surveillance by both the U. S. and British Navies, but no active patrolling or control was undertaken until the Isbrandtsen Lines announced that their ship, *Flying Arrow*, would enter Shanghai. At this point, both the United States and Great Britain established destroyer patrols off Shanghai.

The American destroyers received from their area commander by rapid means voluminous instructions on how to conduct this Patrol and on how to meet every conceivable situation that might be engendered by the actions of *Flying Arrow* and counteraction by the Chinese Nationalist Navy. These instructions were extremely detailed and were enlarged upon almost daily. Soon amplifying instructions were received from the Chief of Naval Operations and the fleet commander involved. Within two days' time, the flood of information and directives had become so great that it was necessary for the patrolling ships to manufacture an index.

After this elaborate preparation, the incident involving *Flying Arrow* was an anticlimax. *Flying Arrow's* actions were not covered by any of the instructions held by the commanding officer of the American destroyer, and, ironically, it became necessary for him to base his decision, not on his instructions, but on International Law and common sense, both of which proved adequate to the situation.

Sometime after the incident, the commanding officers of the groups of American and British destroyers met at a reception in Hong Kong. Discussion naturally turned to the *Flying Arrow* incident, and the subject of International Law and governmental instructions arose. The British commanding officers were astounded at the length and detail of the American instructions. Finally an American commanding officer asked his British counterpart what his instructions had been. Said the British captain, "I had very few. My admiral told me to establish a patrol off Shanghai and when in doubt—*act to protect the Queen's interests.*"

These were his only instructions. His government had given him responsibility with authority and had placed in him a full measure of trust and confidence. The British armed forces have traditionally operated in this fashion. Generally this trust has been given voluntarily, particularly to the Navy, but occasionally it has been necessary for a field commander to remind his Majesty's government of the tradition, as did the Duke of Wellington, who, while campaigning in Spain, found his forces so mired in official correspondence, that he felt compelled to write the following to Lord Beresford, Secretary of State for War:

My Lord,

If I attempted to answer the mass of futile correspondence that surrounds me, I should be debarred from all serious business of campaigning.

I must remind your Lordship—for the last time—that so long as I retain an independent position, I shall see that no officer under my Command is debarred by attending to the futile drivelling of more quill driving in your Lordship's Office—from attending to his first duty—which is, and always has been, so to train the private men under his Command that they may, without question, beat any force opposed to them in the field.

I am, My Lord, Your Obedient Servant, Wellington

Obviously Lord Wellington spoke from that strongest of vantage points, "an independent position." Such a position was the rule rather than the exception in that age of poor communications. Officers were of necessity called upon to execute their country's foreign policy with only the most general guidance. Such a system bred generations of naval officers who were both politically and professionally well informed and who were personally capable of carrying heavy responsibility.

With the advent of rapid communications, however, the necessity for producing such naval officers has diminished, for most problems can be referred to higher echelons of the government for rapid consideration and decision, followed by transmittal of the desired action expected of the commander on the scene.

The British Navy has refused to take this easy path and has determined to retain the atmosphere which produced so many capable naval officers. Rapid communications are used to *inform* the commander on the scene, but not to *direct* him. Such a course of action should continue to produce generations of naval commanders who will be skilled in the exercise of authority and in the discharge of responsibility.

Our Navy can learn a valuable lesson from analysis of this subject. It is not inconceivable that tomorrow's war will start with the destruction or partial disablement of the seat of government and temporary paralysis of communications. Commanders of naval units that survive will face problems not unlike those faced by Drake and Nelson. Effective action will depend upon vigorous and prompt discharge of responsibility by individual commanders all acting in "their country's interest."

Situations of less importance than total war demand the carrying of heavy burdens of responsibility. The commander of the Seventh Fleet, during the first Formosa crisis, shouldered such a burden for a long period of time. The commander of our Sixth Fleet has tremendous responsibility now.

The Problem of Training for Responsibility

Our Navy is fortunate in having trained, over a long period of time, many senior officers to assume responsibility; we will not lack such officers for several years. When these officers retire, however, we will have to depend on the present generation of officers, now in the middle grades, to assume heavy responsibility. There may be doubt in the minds of these officers that they are being trained adequately to meet these responsibilities. Such training must begin early and must become the central theme of the training program for our officer corps. It must offer opportunity for full assumption of authority at early ages, and this authority must be exercised without the fetters of administrative regulation which limit it at the present time.

In many cases our Navy does offer responsibility to officers of the middle grades that is far greater than that given in the past 20 years. Such an example is the responsibility given the young lieutenant who is pilot of a heavy attack, carrier-based aircraft when he is charged with delivering an atomic weapon. In this case, he has the power of decision to deliver (or not to deliver) a military force more than equal to that of the entire fleet a decade ago. The commander of a Polaris submarine has the same power of decision. Today's destroyer commander does not control the same degree of force, but he is given tasks to perform that were considered impossible a generation ago and he is required to carry them out continuously with a crew so relatively inexperienced that he would not have been allowed to take them to sea prior to World War II.

The Nature of Naval Responsibility

Before attacking the problem of improving training in the assumption of responsibility, let us examine briefly the nature of responsibility and its relationship to the naval officer.

No officer can long exercise effective command in any echelon without a thorough understanding of responsibility—its meaning, its limits and, most important, its assumption and exercise. It would seem that every naval officer, by virtue of having chosen the Navy as his profession, would carry responsibility easily, yet some wear it like a weight around their necks, some are afraid of it in any degree, and others seek to hide it or to pass it up or down the chain of command in order to get rid of it.

A competent officer must first be capable of discharging responsibility placed upon him by higher authority. He must understand the limits of the responsibility so given to him and must know when to keep within these and when to exceed them. Secondly, he must be capable of delegating responsibility to his subordinates, and he must understand the necessity of granting sufficient authority to his subordinates in order to allow them to carry out their delegated responsibility. Third, he must also understand the human side of responsibility, particularly as it applies to the unwritten requirements of responsibility sometimes neglected but so necessary for truly effective command. These three basic requirements of responsibility must be mastered by a successful officer and must be mastered so well that they become second nature. To this mastery, a naval officer must add the ability to discharge responsibility with an air of personal enthusiasm and with confidence in his subordinates.

A thoroughly trained naval officer must have instilled in him a positive attitude toward responsibility. He must seek it and assume it readily, completely, and fearlessly. Farragut often said, "I have as much pleasure in running into port in a gale of wind as ever a boy did in a feat of skill." He did not deliberately court danger by entering port during a gale when he could have waited for the storm to abate, but once the necessity was established, he wasted no time pondering the possible consequences of failure on his part. He was known to have been a good enough seaman to take all necessary precautions to insure the safety of his ship and crew in the event that his vessel grounded or broached, but once these preparations were made, he permitted no looking back and no speculation on failure. His crew followed his example and took the wind, the seas, and the rain in the same cheerful spirit that was exhibited by their commander.

Farragut courted responsibility in time of peace, even as a junior commander, and when war came, he was instantly ready to exercise it during his most famous moment when, in spite of cautious suggestions from his subordinates and with only ambiguous instructions from the Navy Department, he took the responsibility of passing the river forts at Vicksburg. Failure might have brought disaster to his cause and to his career, but he refused to be deterred by possible consequences and rose to the occasion with courage and an understanding of the proper exercise of responsibility. He had what Earl St. Vincent declared to be the true test of a man's courage— the power to bear responsibility.

The proper exercise of responsibility does not, however, always manifest itself in such vividly important surroundings as combat or emergency. The successful commander knows that it also must be exercised properly against the more prosaic background of daily routine. He is called upon to spend many days building up the morale of his subordinate commanders and of his men by safeguarding their rights, superintending their education and training, and developing their capabilities.

Every commander must be equally aware at all times of both his responsibility toward his superior and his responsibilities toward his juniors. In the words of William McFee, "Responsibility's like a string we can only see the middle of. Both ends are out of sight." A successful commander must see that responsibility runs straight and true toward both ends of the string. He must indoctrinate and train his subordinates to accept responsibility properly, fully, and fearlessly, and he must guard against censuring or correcting his subordinates in such a way as to impair their readiness and willingness to continue to accept responsibility.

A good ship commander can retire to his sea cabin each night assured of a restful and peaceful night if he is sure his subordinates have been properly trained to accept responsibility, and if he is capable of accepting it himself. Of course, he will have spared no effort in training his watch officers and watchstanders and will have left no doubt in their minds as to his policies and desires. Most importantly, he will have conferred upon them authority commensurate with the responsibility he has given them. Such a commander will reap rich rewards in that he will have a ship that will function efficiently, smartly, and aggressively, whether he is on the bridge or in the sea cabin. He will have followed responsibility straight and true to the bottom of the string.

Toward the top of the string, he must follow a similar method. He must know thoroughly what is required of him by his country, his service—with its multitudinous regulations and requirements—his commander-in-chief, and his seniors in the chain of command. It is not enough that he should know in intimate detail the written regulations setting forth his responsibility and defining its limits. He must understand the fundamental reasons behind these regulations in order that he may interpret and apply them intelligently, and in order that he may successfully meet situations not covered by written regulations. He cannot often go wrong if he follows the method of carrying out regulations advocated by Nelson, who said, "I shall endeavor to comply with all their Lordships directions in such manner as, *to the best of my judgment, will answer their intentions in employing me here.*" Nelson was prepared to accept the responsibility of disobeying the literal word of a written regulation if he thought that he was obeying the spirit behind the regulations.

No human mind can conceive regulations to cover every possible eventuality, and, consequently, a commander is sometimes called upon to act in such a manner as to satisfy the regulations he thinks his service would have made had they been cognizant of the need of such a regulation. Modern technical progress is too rapid for written naval regulations to keep abreast of the resultant changes in naval tactics and techniques. It became apparent that shipboard radar was a foremost aid to navigation long before naval regulations and opinions of the Judge Advocate General decided that a ship possessing radar should be required to operate it in darkness or reduced visibility. Responsible naval commanders early realized this fact and used their radars for navigational purposes as faithfully as if they had been required to do so by law and regulations.

An able and experienced commander will sedulously avoid overworking responsibility. Many commanders seem to find newly assumed command too heady a wine, and in the words of Mahan, "There will always be found at the beginning of a war or upon change of commanders, a restless impatience to do something, to make a showing of results, which misleads the judgment of those in authority, and commonly ends, if not in failure, at least in barren waste of powder and shot." A good commander will always stand out in good time, and a bad one, who tried to hide his faults behind a screen of activity, only makes them more obvious in the end.

This point is equally applicable to the treatment of subordinates. A good commander must expect and demand top performance from his subordinates, but he must not mistake a large amount of activity for successful discharge of responsibility. If his subordinates have exercised foresight and initiative, the result should be a smooth running ship with little outward sign of bustle, hurry, or smoke. A good executive officer is not harried or overworked. If he appears to be so, he is not a good executive and should soon expect correction from his captain, if the latter is a good commander. A commander finding this situation must resist the impulse to return to himself the reins of delegated responsibility and must be of sufficient moral stature to accept the occasional faults of others as normal human error, and should undertake its correction firmly but charitably.

As Franklin D. Roosevelt so aptly stated, "Better the occasional faults of a government that lives in a spirit of charity than the constant omissions of a government frozen in the ice of its own indifference." Mistakes should be expected on the part of subordinates. They should be corrected vigorously and promptly, but in so doing, care should be taken to avoid reducing in even the slightest degree their initiative and eagerness and their taste for responsibility.

The higher echelons of command must preserve in their subordinate commands a healthy attitude toward responsibility. This attitude generally is maintained without difficulty during wartime, when administrative red tape necessarily decreases to a minimum and is subordinated to the successful conduct of war. This is the only attitude toward responsibility that a high commander can afford to promote during wartime. If he were to limit too drastically the responsibility of his subordinate commanders, his mistake would be quickly reflected in a decrease in the performance of duty of his units in their conduct of operations, and in consequence, he would be forced either to restore a healthy attitude toward responsibility or would face censure by his seniors.

After peace comes, however, a faulty attitude toward responsibility is not so readily apparent, and in all ranks there is a tendency to do what is commonly called "keeping your finger on your number." Caution becomes commonplace, replacing aggressiveness and daring, and careful and diligent following of precedent and routine is frequently mistaken for outstanding performance of duty. A commander cannot afford to demonstrate in peacetime that he is aggressive and daring unless he is convinced by his seniors by positive example, statement, and attitude that such characteristics are desired by them.

Fortunately for our country, there is usually at least one highly placed commander in each decade who nurtures and preserves a proper attitude toward responsibility. Prior to the First World War, Admiral Sims lifted our destroyer service from the doldrums with a magnificent correspondence endorsement that was soon well known to all destroyer captains, and it is quoted in full as an example of a full understanding of the relation between command and responsibility.

> Boats so delicate, which, to be handled effectively must be handled
> with great daring, necessarily run great risks, and their commanders
> must, of course, realize that a prerequisite to successfully handling

them is the willingness to run such risks. That they will observe proper precautions is, of course, required, but it is more important that our officers should handle these boats with dash and daring than that the boats should be kept unscratched. There must be developed in the men that handle them that mixture of skill and daring which can only be attained if the boats are habitually used under circumstances which imply the risk of accident. The business of a naval officer is one which above all others, needs daring and decision, and if he must err on either side, the nation can best afford to have him err on the side of too much daring rather than too much caution.

No destroyer commander who had read this statement could fail to understand perfectly what was required of him, and it is a matter of proud record that they carried out their responsibilities accordingly.

It is unfortunately true that responsibility is not always assumed and understood by all in the echelons of command as well as it was assumed and understood by Admiral Sims. A subordinate commander can only prepare for the worst and then resolutely hope for the best. He must think more of the success of his work for the sake of his work if he is to enjoy peace of mind. If he assumes responsibility readily, he may someday encounter a superior who does not entertain responsibility with pleasure and who will probably not fully appreciate the effort of his subordinate, particularly if the subordinate is so unfortunate as to commit an error while assuming more responsibility or authority than the superior thinks he should have had. In time of peace, one such adverse circumstance can lead to a failure to be selected for promotion, but it is worth much more in personal satisfaction to be set down for an error of commission than to be promoted merely because the selection board can find nothing in your record to show that you have done anything either right or wrong.

There are inherent in our Navy's traditions, methods of training, and command policy all the elements necessary for the proper training of officers in the assumption of responsibility and the exercise of authority. We need only to preserve and to nurture these elements to assure that they are not forgotten or derogated. We, individually and collectively, need to take positive action to accomplish this task.

We need to re-affirm our intent to continue to couple authority and responsibility and to maintain maximum freedom of action for our commanders on every level of command.

On the levels of command above our service, we must take the lead in implementing reorganization, and we must do so enthusiastically, and completely. We must make available to the other services our long tradition of flexibility in command and we must work to be sure other services which have not had this advantage are not able to control or dominate command arrangements in such a manner that flexibility can be denied to joint commanders.

Within our own service we must work to enhance the status of command. We have been guilty since World War II of decreasing the flexibility we used to accord to our commanding officers. In an attempt to standardize and to provide guidance, we have released a flood of directives from all levels on many subjects. The result is a mass of instructions and notices which limit rather than help a commanding officer. A successful attack must be made on this problem.

On lower levels we can restore the traditional importance of the chief petty officer by returning to him the position of responsibility he once had. This could be accomplished by removing from the chain of command above him all the young ensigns who are now assigned as junior division officers immediately upon reporting. These young officers do not have sufficient practical knowledge to exercise command until they have received functional training and shipboard indoctrination. Exercising command without this knowledge reduces their prestige in the eyes of enlisted personnel and makes difficult the position of chief and leading petty officers in the chain of command. One alternative would be to hold such officers in a training status and not regularly assign them to divisions until they have attained the practical knowledge and information necessary to enable them to carry out the full responsibilities of a junior division officer.

There are many other areas in which we can make progress. The knowledge that the Navy is interested in methods to accomplish these purposes will stimulate ideas.

The Final Goal

We must work actively to preserve our naval tradition of command flexibility both against external attempts to force us into a common mold of over-regulated mediocrity and against internal carelessness.

We must make this effort on all command levels, but most importantly, a proper understanding of responsibility as we understand it must be implanted in all young naval officers at the beginning of their naval education. This concept must be nurtured by the Navy and enhanced and developed by the individual officer as he continues his career. Much can be learned from observation of successful commanders and from our Navy's present competent command and staff schools. It is the duty of every officer who aspires to be a successful commander to make himself proficient in the recognition, assumption, and discharge of responsibility, both toward his superiors and toward his subordinates. He must learn to meet his responsibility eagerly and enthusiastically, to seek it out, and having found it, to live with it easily, fearlessly, and intimately. If he is successful in these efforts, he will wear the heavy mantle of command lightly and with continuing success.

8 "ADMIRAL KING AND THE NAVAL HIGH COMMAND"

FADM Ernest J. King, USN, and
CDR Walter Muir Whitehill, USNR

World War II is arguably the pinnacle of the U.S. Navy's history in terms of combat and worldwide theater operations. It therefore offers an excellent case study in the art and science of command.

This revealing account of the establishment of the U.S. Navy's high command structure at the beginning of World War II is noteworthy not only for its historical significance but also as an examination into the mind of one of the ablest commanders in the Navy's history. This article appeared in *Proceedings* in October 1952 as a preview chapter from a forthcoming book, *Fleet Admiral King, A Naval Record*, by King and his coauthor that was published by W. W. Norton & Company later that year.

Admiral King was serving as commander in chief of the U.S. Atlantic Fleet at the outbreak of the war but was subsequently appointed commander in chief of the U.S Fleet (COMINCH) and Chief of Naval Operations (CNO). Serving for the duration of the war, he wielded more command authority over the U.S. Navy than any admiral before or since.

"ADMIRAL KING AND THE NAVAL HIGH COMMAND"

By FADM Ernest J. King, USN, and CDR Walter Muir Whitehill, USNR, U.S. Naval Institute *Proceedings* (October 1952): 1073–79.

On Monday, 8 December 1941, King received orders by telephone to come to Washington the following day. Shortly after noon on Tuesday the erroneous report of an air raid on New York was received at Newport, and *Augusta* went to general quarters. Lieutenant Commander Harry Sanders, the aide who was to accompany King on his journey, passed the word concerning the raid and was told, "That will not influence our plans." So he and King left *Augusta* about two o'clock, in civilian clothes, and drove to Kingston, Rhode Island, where they boarded the afternoon express from Boston that brought them to Washington shortly before midnight.

King remained at the Navy Department until Saturday, 13 December, when he returned to his flagship. Secretary Knox had left Washington for Pearl Harbor on the ninth, while King was on his way down from Newport. On the fourteenth the Secretary got back to Washington with firsthand knowledge of the condition of the United States Pacific Fleet, and with the conviction that a "new deal" in naval command was imperative. As a result of his recommendations, the President, on 17 December, relieved Admiral H. E. Kimmel from active service in the Navy, and designated Admiral C. W. Nimitz, Chief of the Bureau of Naval Personnel, as Commander in Chief, United States Pacific Fleet.[1] King was once again summoned to Washington, and, arriving Tuesday morning, 16 December, was immediately confronted by Mr. Knox with the proposition of becoming Commander in Chief, United States Fleet. That afternoon at half-past four, accompanied by Admiral Stark, he was taken to the White House by the Secretary, and two days later, on the eighteenth, President Roosevelt issued Executive Order 8984 "Prescribing the Duties of the Commander in Chief of the United States Fleet and the Cooperative Duties of the Chief of Naval Operations."

Among the many decisions made by the President in the early days of the war, few had a more telling effect upon the operation of the United States Navy than the one which led to the issuing of Executive Order 8984. This order stemmed from the realization that for the purpose of exercising command all oceans must be regarded as one area, to the end that effective coordinated control and the proper distribution of our naval power might be realized. It provided that the Commander in Chief, United States Fleet "shall have supreme command of the operating forces comprising the several fleets of the United States Navy and the operating forces of the Naval Coastal Frontier Command, and shall be directly responsible, under the general direction of the Secretary of the Navy, to the President of the United States therefor." The order further directed:

> The staff of the Commander in Chief, United States Fleet shall be composed of a Chief of Staff and of such officers and agencies as appropriate and necessary to perform duties in general as follows:
>
> (a) Make available for evaluation all pertinent information and naval intelligence;
> (b) Prepare and execute plans for current war operations;
> (c) Conduct operational duties;
> (d) Effect all essential communications;
> (e) Direct training essential to carrying out operations;
> (f) Serve as personal aides.

The Commander in Chief shall keep the Chief of Naval Operations informed of the logistic and other needs of the operating forces, and in turn the Chief of Naval Operations shall keep the Commander in Chief informed as to the extent to which the various needs can be met. Subject to the foregoing, the duties and responsibilities of the Chief of Naval Operations under the Secretary of the Navy will remain unchanged. The Chief of Naval Operations shall continue to be responsible for the preparation of war plans from the long range point of view.

In order that close liaison may be maintained with the Navy Department, the principal office of the Commander in Chief shall be in the Navy Department, unless otherwise directed.

A radical change in naval administration was accomplished by this order. As will be recalled from earlier chapters, the authority of the Chief of Naval Operations, having never been precisely defined, had been the subject of much controversy and deliberation. The 1915 legislation creating the office had provided that he "shall, under the direction of the Secretary, be charged with the operations of the fleet, and with the preparation and readiness of plans for its use in war." But neither this law, nor any subsequent one, had given him authority over the bureaus of the Navy Department that built, manned, supplied, and maintained the fleet. During more than a quarter of a century the great majority of Chiefs of Naval Operations had felt the inconsistency of this situation, and had become convinced that the powers of the office should extend over the activities of the bureaus. Their view was based upon the administrative principle that the office entrusted with responsibility for the efficiency of the fleet should not be dependent upon the operations of various independent agencies, each of which contribute directly to the fleet. The previous Chiefs of Naval Operations had correctly diagnosed the deficiencies of their office, and had made frequent recommendations to the Secretary of the Navy to correct them. These recommendations had not been adopted.

With the outbreak of the war, prompt action to remedy the organizational deficiencies of the Office of the Chief of Naval Operations became essential. The concept of a Commander in Chief, United States Fleet, separate and distinct from, and in addition to the other three commanders in chief afloat, was consequently seized upon to designate the functions to be carried out by the head of the operating forces, and the Headquarters, Commander in Chief, United States Fleet was established in the Navy Department in Washington to fulfill some of the functions that the peacetime Chief of Naval Operations should have had under his control.

On 20 December the President designated King as Commander in Chief, United States Fleet. Having come back to Newport on the nineteenth to wind up his affairs in the Atlantic Fleet, he left *Augusta* on the twentieth, by plane from Quonset, for Washington, and did not return again. *Vixen*, the flagship of Rear Admiral Richard S. Edwards, Commander Submarines, Atlantic Fleet, having been lent for King's temporary use, came alongside *Augusta* at Newport, took on King's papers and belongings, and got under way for the Washington Navy Yard.

With the establishment in Washington of the headquarters of the Commander in Chief, United States Fleet (abbreviated to COMINCH rather than the traditional CINCUS, which after 7 December, appeared to have undesirable connotations), King brought ashore the concept of a fleet staff. Many of the principles that had been evolved in the Atlantic in 1941, as well as certain of the personnel that had assisted him in their application, were transferred to the new organization. It was necessary to act with the greatest possible speed and precision, for the urgency of the military situation left no time for leisurely planning and experimentation. King was obliged to create COMINCH headquarters practically out of nothing. Everything had to be accomplished in the minimum time, for in December 1941 the most essential thing from the operational viewpoint was that what remained of the fleet should be so disposed that it could continue in useful existence while the industrial strength of the country was being mobilized.

Space was hastily cleared on the third floor of the Navy Department Building on Constitution Avenue, immediately above the rooms traditionally occupied by the Chief of Naval Operations. Captain F. S. Low, Commander R. E. Libby, and Lieutenant C. B. Lanman, who had been members of King's staff in the Atlantic Fleet, received orders on 24 December to report to Washington "as soon as may be," were detached on Christmas Day, and presented themselves on the twenty-seventh. They were soon followed by Commander George C. Dyer and Commander George L. Russell, who set about establishing the most essential services. Rear Admiral Russell Willson, Superintendent of the Naval Academy and a shipmate of King's thirty years earlier on Rear Admiral Osterhaus's staff, was summoned by telephone from Annapolis to become Chief of Staff, and as Deputy Chief of Staff, Rear Admiral Richard S. Edwards came from New London. As Edwards subsequently recalled the situation:

Upon my arrival in Washington on 29 December I found Admiral King enthroned in the most disreputable office I have ever seen. Someone had moved out in a hurry, taking the furniture with him, but not the dirt. The Admiral had liberated a flat top desk from somewhere and a couple of chairs. He sat on one side of the desk, opposite him sat Russell Willson (the Chief of Staff). I and my assistant (Captain F. S. Low) borrowed a broken down table from a friend who was out to lunch and set up shop in a corner of the Admiral's office. The Admiral had brought some aides, a flag secretary and a collection of yeomen from the Atlantic Fleet; they were putting together a secretariat and a communications section. The old War Plans Division of CNO was operating as the Planning Section of the Staff. That was all there was. I recall thinking that as the headquarters of the greatest navy in the world it fell somewhat short of being impressive.

King had relatively little time, however, to enjoy the amenities of this unswept office, for shortly before Christmas the Prime Minister of Great Britain and certain of his staff came to Washington to confer with the President and the American military leaders. The meetings of the ARCADIA Conference, which extended from 24 December to 14 January 1942, required King's attendance. In addition to such considerations of international strategy, there was pressing need of reconciling plans for the immediate future in the Pacific with the resources available after the Pearl Harbor attack. On Christmas Day King asked that an immediate study be made for a fueling base in the South Pacific.

It was 30 December 1941 before King was formally detached from duty as Commander in Chief, United States Atlantic Fleet, and assumed the duties of Commander in Chief, United States Fleet. At noon that day his flag was hoisted in U.S.S. *Vixen* at the Navy Yard, Washington. His first act was to send a dispatch to Admiral Nimitz, who had by then arrived in Pearl Harbor, summarizing the two primary tasks assigned him:

(1) Covering and holding the Hawaii-Midway line and maintaining its communications with the west coast.

(2) Maintaining communications between the west coast and Australia, chiefly by covering, securing and holding the Hawaii-Samoa line, which should be extended to include Fiji at the earliest practicable date.

Admiral Thomas C. Hart, the Commander in Chief, United States Asiatic Fleet, was informed by dispatch on 31 December that the strategic policy for the Far East (agreed upon by the United States and British Chiefs of Staff) was to hold the Malay Barrier as the basic defensive position; to operate forces in depth forward of the Barrier to check Japanese advances; to hold Burma and Australia as supporting positions; to support the Philippines; to maintain essential communications in the theater. Furthermore, the need of close cooperation among British, Dutch, and United States commanders was indicated.

In establishing headquarters in Washington, many basic policies that King had learned from Admiral Mayo during World War I, and had in turn followed during his command of the Atlantic Fleet, were applied to the new emergency. Here, more than ever before, was a situation requiring decentralization and the encouragement of intelligent initiative of the subordinate. Here too was the supreme test of making the best of what he had, for, in all conscience, King had little enough to work with!

Although Executive Order 8984 had not specifically established the relationship between the new Commander in Chief, United States Fleet, and the Chief of Naval Operations, it was obvious that certain functions formerly in the office of the latter would have to be transferred to the new COMINCH headquarters. The post of Commander in Chief, United States Fleet was considered as duty afloat, and in view of the possibility that King might wish to go to sea at any time, provision was made in all planning for a staff that could accompany him with little warning. It was consequently essential that this staff establish correspondence and communications files that were entirely independent of any previously existing in the Navy Department.

In January 1942 certain sections of the Office of the Chief of Naval Operations were transferred bodily, with their personnel, to King's headquarters, and the necessary readjustments were made with a high degree of cooperation and good feeling on the part of Admiral Stark. In questions that arose concerning the relationship between the old and the new commands, King personally stood up for the concept that Commander in Chief, United States Fleet should be under the Chief of Naval Operations, but was overruled in this by the President and the Secretary of the Navy.

When first confronted by Secretary Knox in mid-December 1941 with the proposal that he become Commander in Chief, United States Fleet, King had demurred, saying that in his opinion the functions involved belonged under the Chief of Naval Operations. Upon the Secretary's insistence, however, he had acquiesced. The demarcation of authority in this joint consulship of Stark and King was never clearly defined. Between the men themselves there were strong ties of friendship, good will, and mutual desire to make the best of what they had. Nevertheless, the ambiguous relationship of a Chief of Naval Operations, traditionally responsible for certain functions, and a Commander in Chief, United States Fleet—brought ashore contrary to all previous precedent and made "directly responsible" to the President—led to confusion not only in the Navy Department but in other branches of government. It was not always clear what lay in Stark's province and what in King's.

From time to time King commented upon the necessity of a clearer command relationship between COMINCH and CNO, and on one occasion, when at the White House with Secretary Knox, he spoke to the President concerning this, pointing out that a definite relationship should be established, that he as COMINCH was perfectly willing to be under CNO, and in fact thought that the logical arrangement. The President indicated that he and the Secretary would take care of that situation. It was eventually taken care of in a manner that King had neither sought to bring about nor anticipated, for in March 1942 the President determined that Admiral Stark should go to London as Commander, U.S. Naval Forces, Europe.

This was one consequence of Pearl Harbor that mystified King. He had felt that the Roberts Commission[2] had not reached the heart of the matter, but had merely produced scapegoats to satisfy the popular demand for fixing the responsibility for the Pearl Harbor debacle. It had seemed to him that Admiral

Kimmel and General Short had been sacrificed to political expediency, and that Admiral Stark was now suffering the same fate. As Chief of Naval Operations, Stark's position in relation to the Pearl Harbor attack was less responsible than that of General Marshall as Chief of Staff of the Army. By an arrangement of many years standing (approved by the Joint Board and by the Secretaries of War and the Navy), the Army was responsible for the land defenses of the Hawaiian Islands, including the security of Pearl Harbor and ships in port there, just as it had always been responsible for the defense of all United States harbors and ports. The failure of the Army, and especially of the Air Corps, to discharge their responsibilities was—to King's disgust—carefully glossed over during the investigation. King has never been able to reconcile the difference in the President's treatment of Admiral Stark and General Marshall in regard to Pearl Harbor. While General Marshall was allowed to remain in Washington as Chief of Staff of the Army, Admiral Stark suffered a demotion in being sent to London, where during the remainder of the war, he rendered important services to the Allied cause.

On 12 March President Roosevelt issued Executive Order 9096 providing that "the duties of Commander in Chief, United States Fleet and the duties of the Chief of Naval Operations may be combined and devolve upon one officer who shall have the title 'Commander in Chief, United States Fleet, and Chief of Naval Operations' and who shall be the principal naval adviser and executive to the Secretary of the Navy on the conduct of the Naval Establishment." This order specified that:

> As Commander in Chief, United States Fleet, the officer holding the combined offices as herein provided shall have supreme command of the operating forces comprising the several fleets, seagoing forces, and sea frontier forces of the United States Navy and shall be directly responsible, under the general direction of the Secretary of the Navy, to the President therefor.
>
> As Chief of Naval Operations, the officer holding the combined offices as herein provided shall be charged, under the direction of the Secretary of the Navy, with the preparation, readiness, and logistic

support of the operating forces comprising the several fleets, seagoing forces and sea frontier forces of the United States Navy, and with the coordination and direction of effort to this end of the bureaus and offices of the Navy Department except such offices (other than bureaus) as the Secretary of the Navy may specifically exempt. Duties as Chief of Naval Operations shall be contributory to the discharge of the paramount duties of Commander in Chief, United States Fleet.

The order further provided that the staff of Commander in Chief, United States Fleet should consist of a Chief of Staff with such Deputy and Assistant Chiefs of Staff as might be necessary, and that the staff of the Chief of Naval Operations should be composed of a Vice Chief of Naval Operations, a Sub Chief, and such additional Assistant Chiefs and other officers as might be required. In compliance with this Executive Order,[3] King relieved Stark on 26 March 1942 and assumed duty as Chief of Naval Operations, while Vice Admiral F. J. Horne became Vice Chief of Naval Operations. Horne knew the ropes, for he had had three months of wartime experience since December 1941 in the Office of the Chief of Naval Operations as Stark's principal assistant.[4]

Throughout the war, however, the organizations of Headquarters, Commander in Chief, United States Fleet and the Office of the Chief of Naval Operations were maintained separately and distinctly, the two activities being united only in the persons of Admiral King and (after October 1944) of Admiral Edwards, who was at that time appointed Deputy COMINCH-Deputy CNO.

In March 1942 about eighty-five officers were on duty in COMINCH headquarters, and, though the number grew, every effort was made to keep it low. King wished to maintain a small, closely knit organization that could function effectively, and he was continually vigilant to avoid any excesses of personnel or the development of useless functions. All proposals for any kind of expansion required convincing justification, while King's intolerance of incompetence effectively prevented any flowering of bureaucracy.

In selecting personnel, great care was exercised to obtain officers of high abilities who were fresh from direct contact with the sea-going forces. The first to report came from the Atlantic Fleet. Later, officers were chosen who had been successful in combat in all theaters, and who would thus collectively avoid the dangers of overemphasis on any one ocean or area.[5] King insisted upon a continuous turnover, so as to keep his headquarters free of the "Washington mentality," and with a very few exceptions (such as Admirals Willson, Edwards, and C. M. Cooke, who were necessarily frozen in their important duties throughout the war)[6] few senior officers remained in headquarters over a year.

Experienced chief petty officers, many of whom were later commissioned, junior Reserve officers, and afterward WAVES [Women Accepted for Voluntary Emergency Service]—both commissioned and enlisted—who were extensively and successfully used for watch standing and secretarial duties, remained for longer periods and formed a dependable backlog, but the fleet point of view was consistently maintained by the constant arrival of officers with active combat experience.

Because of these considerations, Headquarters, Commander in Chief, United States Fleet preserved throughout the war a certain seagoing character quite unfamiliar to Washington. The organization started from scratch with the war. There was no book in which to look for answers. There were no civilian employees with fixed habits to consider. "Empire builders" were conspicuous by their absence. Business *had* to be conducted with the maximum of efficiency and speed, and so entirely pragmatic methods were evolved which worked because of the personal characters of the officers carrying them out.

Notes

1. As Nimitz was then in Washington and could not reach Pearl Harbor for some days, King's old friend Vice Admiral W. S. Pye, Commander Battle Force, was designated as Commander in Chief, United States Pacific Fleet pro tem.

2. This commission, organized under an Executive Order of 18 December 1941, with Mr. Justice Owen J. Roberts, United States Supreme Court, as chairman, began its inquiry immediately and concluded it on 23 January 1942.

3. Both Executive Orders 8984 and 9096 were drafted by Rear Admirals W. R. Sexton and J. O. Richardson, of the General Board, and King had no hand in their composition beyond introducing into the March order the statement that "duties as Chief of Naval Operations shall be contributory to the discharge of

the paramount duties of Commander in Chief, United States Fleet."

4.   In December 1941, when King was appointed COMINCH, the question of his relief in the Atlantic Fleet had to be decided immediately. In the fall of 1941 it had been Stark's idea that, in the event of war, King would remain in command of the Atlantic Fleet, that Nimitz would go to the Asiatic Fleet, while Rear Admiral R. E. Ingersoll, then Stark's principal assistant, would go to the Pacific. When King came to Washington as Commander in Chief, United States Fleet, Secretary Knox had already decided that Nimitz would relieve Kimmel in command of the Pacific Fleet. The days of the Asiatic Fleet were so obviously numbered that there was no need of anyone going out there, and it therefore seemed logical and inevitable that Ingersoll should relieve King in the Atlantic. However, when King proposed this to Stark, Stark demurred, saying that Ingersoll was indispensable in the office of the Chief of Naval Operations. King insisted that Ingersoll was so able a man as to be necessary at sea, and suggested that either Rear Admiral Russell Willson or Rear Admiral Horne would make a suitable assistant. He further proposed that Stark choose the one of these two officers whom he preferred as a replacement for Ingersoll and that he, King, would then take the other for his chief of staff. Stark agreed that Ingersoll should go as Commander in Chief, United States Atlantic Fleet, and chose Horne as his assistant. Consequently, Russell Willson became King's chief of staff. Horne continued as Vice Chief of Naval Operations throughout the war.

5.   For example, Commander Howard E. Orem, who relieved Captain G. L. Russell as flag secretary in 1943, had (as executive officer of a cruiser and as chief of Staff to the commander of a task force) in less than two years of war been in the Atlantic, the South Pacific, the North Pacific, served with the British Home Fleet, and participated in the bitterly attacked north Russian convoy PQ-17. King's flag lieutenants were usually young and cocky submarine commanders, brought ashore for well-deserved change of duty after the completion of several successful war patrols in the far reaches of the Pacific.

6.   In August 1942 Russell Willson was retired for physical disability, and after a short period as Deputy Commander in Chief, United States Fleet, became the Navy member of the Joint Strategic Survey Committee of the Joint Chiefs of Staff. His successor as King's Chief of Staff was Richard S. Edwards, a remarkable man who combined penetrating intellectual abilities of the highest order with an immense capacity for hard work. Although Edwards earnestly desired to go to sea, the state of his health would not permit it, and so he

remained as King's principal assistant throughout the war. At all times extremely valuable, at some times well-nigh indispensable, Edwards lightened the most complicated problems by the seemingly effortless sallies of a genuine wit, worthy of Will Rogers. Although his name is hardly known to the American public, Edwards is one of the outstanding flag officers of the United States Navy. When in September 1944 he became Deputy Commander in Chief, United States Fleet and Deputy Chief of Naval Operations, he was succeeded as Chief of Staff by Vice Admiral Charles M. Cooke, Jr. Cooke—nicknamed "Savvy" for good reason—had served in the Plans Division of Naval Operations before the war, had been sent by Stark to the Pacific in 1941 as commanding officer of the Pacific Fleet flagship Pennsylvania, and had been brought back to Washington by King in June 1942 as Assistant Chief of Staff (Plans). In October 1943 he became Deputy Chief of Staff. Cooke, whose turn of mind made him uncommonly useful in planning future operations, usually accompanied King on his journeys overseas, while Edwards, whose poor health prevented him from flying, held the fort in Washington. Although King felt that Cooke, for the sake of his own career, should return to sea after two years in Washington, Cooke, with Edwards's approval, unselfishly chose to remain throughout the war with King, who was grateful for his many valuable services.

9 "A FLAGSHIP VIEW OF COMMAND DECISIONS"

CAPT Gilven M. Slonim, USN

In April 1958 Captain Slonim presented his "observations during some intensely interesting command decisions at sea in the Pacific War," making it clear that "the observations developed are based primarily on personal experience rather than research." He was well-positioned for those observations, having served on several key staffs during the war, including the Chief of Naval Operations; the commander in chief, Pacific Fleet; and the commanders of the Third and Fifth Fleets.

With real-world, high-intensity operations as his catalyst, Captain Slonim provides some practical guidance for the achievement of effective command.

"A FLAGSHIP VIEW OF COMMAND DECISIONS"

By CAPT Gilven M. Slonim, USN, U.S. Naval Institute *Proceedings* (April 1958): 80–91.

Collapsing into a chair in the *Saratoga's* Flag Plot in the moments following the Stewart Island action, Admiral Fletcher said: "Boys, I'm going to get two dispatches tonight, one from Admiral Nimitz telling me what a wonderful job we did, and one from King saying 'Why in hell didn't you use your destroyers and make torpedo attacks?' and by God, they'll both be right." This rather interesting anecdote is apt illustration of the fact that there are no *absolutes* in the field of "Command Decisions." Students of naval warfare have considered the subject of naval command decisions a particularly fascinating one. This article was written to present my observations during some intensely interesting command decisions at sea in the Pacific War. The observations developed are based primarily on personal experience rather than research, and it is well appreciated that they fall short of completeness.

The subject of command decisions has received some rather censorious treatment in the past by various experts of varying degrees of expertness. Were a composite recorded of all criticism thrust upon military commanders throughout history, one might, on the basis of such compilation, deduce that no military man in the history of warfare—land, naval, or air—ever made a truly sound decision. This, of course, simply wouldn't be true. As a matter of fact, the naval war in the Pacific, the arena of our experience, affords many historic examples of brilliant and spectacular military decisions. The primary objective of the author is not to pass judgment on these decisions, but rather to analyze them to determine what each can contribute to a more comprehensive knowledge of the basic ingredients of sound decisions at sea.

Readers of the PROCEEDINGS in particular recognize that the basis of professional existence of military officers is primarily that of preparation for command and the exercise of such in an effective manner. Military officers strive principally to train themselves to make sound command decisions and appreciate that their ultimate success or failure will rest primarily on their ability to do so competently, provided they are fortunate enough to have the opportunity.

One element that the "experts" often fail to consider in their critiques is the "atmosphere" in which decisions at sea, or military decisions for that matter, are made. The whizzing sound of bullets and multifarious and perplexing factors compound the difficulties inherent in arriving at sound decisions. These agitators are ebullient gremlins assiduously creating the well-known "fog of war," and they detract appreciably from a peace of mind approach to making tactical decisions. They are of particular importance if one is to recapture the atmosphere in which decisions were made. Further, it is my conviction that no major Task Force or Fleet Commander ever had sufficient intelligence (in the military sense of that word!) to insure that his decisions could be made with absolute certainty. For these reasons, it seems imperative that a realistic background atmosphere be related to any analysis of the following interesting decisions.

This article includes several of the operations in the Pacific which the author witnessed and in which he had the good fortune to participate. The Pacific War decisions were not selected on the basis of their momentous effect on the ultimate outcome of the war, but because each brings out some interesting points on Pacific War decisions. For example, the Marcus Island raid had no effect in changing the over-all complexion of the war; yet it is consistent with our selected criteria by virtue of its fascinating nature.

Marcus Island Raid

The raid commenced with a dispatch—most operations did. Subsequent to the second raid on Wake Island, Admiral Halsey received a dispatch from Admiral Nimitz stating his desire that a raid be conducted against Marcus Island. If memory serves, an escape clause was included within the dispatch directive, such as "if feasible" or "if practicable." But the intention of the Commander in Chief of the Pacific Fleet was quite apparent; he wanted the raid carried out. Several members of the Staff were with Admiral Halsey in the *Enterprise*'s Flag Plot when this dispatch was received. After observing the location of Marcus some 960 miles southwest of Tokyo, wrestling with the destroyer logistic problem involved, and contemplating the number of aircraft in the *Enterprise* Air Group, Admiral Halsey was somehow able to restrain his enthusiasm for the operation. It was obvious that he, the Master of the Raid, must employ an entirely new type of striking operation. Here was a genuine challenge!

To analyze the problem area of the decision, two questions appear salient: Can this raid be conducted, and if so, how? Now, we recall that contemporaneous to the Marcus Raid the Fleet was "shadow boxing" with a profusion of

Japanese "ghosts." There was a great deal of concern with the submarine infested waters of the Pacific, and we had almost an unduly great respect for the unknown in our approach to the Japanese submarine potential. Marcus, less than a thousand miles from Tokyo, still gave one a feeling of "messing around" in the enemy's backyard. The actual conduct of the raid is particularly noteworthy in point of courage and imagination which Admiral Halsey demonstrated in executing Admiral Nimitz's directive, even though his initial reaction to the projected operation lacked enthusiasm. This operation may have been the impetus for the "Swim With Halsey Club" which was organized about that time aboard the carrier *Enterprise*. As it developed, the Marcus Island raid was conducted by the *Enterprise* and two cruisers, the *Salt Lake City* and the *Northampton*. In view of the short-leggedness of the destroyers, the decision was made to leave the destroyer screen behind with the tanker. Unquestionably, this raid was the inception of the operational requirement for the nuclear destroyer. Consider how much less perplexing this tactical decision for the strike would have been for Admiral Halsey were his screen composed of nuclear "cans," so that it was feasible to take his destroyers with him!

There is a sidelight in connection with the Marcus Raid which is rather interesting. We listened continuously to the Japanese radio station on Marcus Island. The weather had been unfavorable at the launching point after our approach, and quite understandably there was some anxious conjecture concerning the weather which would be encountered over the target during the conduct of the strike. As a matter of fact, the first launch of the *Enterprise* Air Group was delayed in the hope that most positive information of weather at the target would be available before ordering the carrier aircraft to take off. Fortunately the Japanese were extremely co-operative. Their broadcast station "joined the air" promptly at five o'clock and commenced the day with a forecast of the local weather, indicating the Oriental weather prophet felt suitable atmospheric conditions would be provided for the bombing of the Islands. Upon receipt of this information, the strike was immediately launched. In most instances the enemy was not so generous in sharing the work of their weatherman as were the Japanese in this operation.

The Marcus Island raid is unique in that it involves no command relationship problems. There were no contact report problems similar to those which recur constantly in later operations. The raid was conducted without further incident. One aircraft was lost, but considerable damage was inflicted on the air installations, which impeded the Japanese shuttle of aircraft to the Marshall and Gilbert Islands. But perhaps most importantly, the success of the raid quite conceivably provided a germ for Japanese thinking toward more defensive air employments. It may well have been the starting point for the enemy's husbanding resources for the defense of their Empire. Quite probably Admiral Nimitz's purpose in conducting this raid was to "obtain a sounding" on the effectiveness of the Japanese defense of their homeland in preparation for ensuing operation. In any case, the conduct of this Task Force operation emphasizes determination, as characterized by Admiral Halsey, as an important component of the sound decision. Determination, here as always, is apparent as an essential element of effective leadership in action.

The Doolittle Raid

The Doolittle raid provides some interesting food for thought on the subject of the problems faced by the man in command at sea, at the point of contact. As planned and agreed upon, the Doolittle Strike was expected to be a rather uncomplicated affair. There were no illusions of grandeur regarding the raid. Admiral Halsey was to move in Task Force Sixteen to some six hundred miles off Japan's coast, launch Doolittle, and get out. There were but two carriers and a minimum of heavy support ships and destroyers for the screen. With B-25's spotted on deck and U.S. Army Air Corps pilots and crews aboard, the *Hornet*, with Doolittle embarked, sailed from a United States port, while aboard the *Enterprise* Admiral Halsey sortied his Task Group out of Pearl Harbor in preparation for a rendezvous north of Midway with the *Hornet* Task Group. Almost immediately upon joining up, Halsey received a dispatch from Doolittle. Perhaps the dispatch warrants close scrutiny; it is an extremely interesting message in point of tactics. Now it must be remembered that the launching point agreed upon by Halsey and Doolittle, at a secret conference in San Francisco prior to undertaking the mission, was to be six hundred miles due east of Tokyo, the center of the Mikado' might. In his dispatch to Halsey, Doolittle pointed out that from a position six hundred miles off the coast he felt that he had very little chance of effectively conducting his strike and also enabling his pilots to return safely to the prearranged air bases in China during daylight. "From five hundred miles my chances would be much improved," he stated. However, he felt that in order to ensure an effective strike and the safe return of his pilots, he would prefer a launch point four hundred miles off the coast of Japan. This he felt was the safe range, and the best range from his point of view. Doolittle was, of course, seeking the optimum in effective range for his raid. Whether these facts are commonly known is not certain. One must admire Doolittle immensely for the imagination, the courage, and the capability he demonstrated in designing the operation, then selling and executing it himself. It was Doolittle's dream. He was prepared to see it through, regardless of the odds.

Obviously the crux of Admiral Halsey's decision was the determination of the optimum launch point. There was a problem of time and distance involved in the task of getting Doolittle in, then getting the Striking Force out. The Doolittle dispatch, in effect, changed the complexion of the entire operation for Admiral Halsey. For all practical purposes he had to "start all over again"—the objective, the risk, the threat, the tactics—all required a new, but quick look. As Task Force Commander, he was obliged to make a decision based upon a further evaluation of the tactical situation, requiring that he re-analyze such prime factors as the relative security of his small force compared with possible losses of Doolittle's aircraft. CINCPAC had thoroughly briefed Admiral Halsey, prior to his departure from Pearl, on the probable reception he would receive were his forces to draw too near to the coast of Japan. The warmth of the Shinto reaction to be expected was stressed in this briefing. *Yamato Damashi*, as the true samurai spirit, quite probably would be encountered in the initial direct action against the Empire. Every aircraft capable of carrying a bomb or torpedo would be loosed against his forces and ordered to "attack and destroy the enemy." Admiral Halsey's superb ability as a great leader and fighter is widely recognized. He was, of course, extremely anxious to do all he could to meet Doolittle's request in this operation. They arrived at a compromise acceptable to Doolittle which appears to have been very sound. Admiral Halsey agreed to exert all efforts to take Doolittle in to four hundred miles from the coast of Japan to ensure the success of his over-all operation even though the previously agreed position had been six hundred miles. But recognizing the existing military threats and particularly that of shore based air, he felt that if the Force were sighted and reported at any time he would be obliged to direct an immediate launch of the Doolittle strikes.

We all know what happened. When the Task Force had penetrated to but eight hundred miles off the coast, it encountered several small patrol craft of the Japanese Fifth Fleet. These "Spit kits" were a part of a mobile defense line that guarded the final approaches to Japan. The ships of this group were assigned primary duties of reporting the enemy and their collateral task was fishing. The *Nashville* opened fire on the first of these units but was unable to sink it expediently. Whether or not our force had been reported was of course the immediate question. We had picked up some rather frantic and garbled Japanese conversation which understandably evidenced extreme anxiety. Captain Buraker, the Operations Officer, called to ask if the Japanese had reported our presence, and we told him we were reasonably certain that they had. Thereupon Admiral Halsey directed that Doolittle be launched. Very shortly thereafter the Civil Air Defense circuits in the Empire teemed with forewarning messages, confirming our assumption. We had been sighted and reported, and the Empire was alerted for our attack! We believed that 70,000,000 Japanese, heretofore thoroughly impressed with their invincibility by constant reports of their successes and impressive results of their offensive actions from Pearl Harbor to Singapore, now awaited somewhat stunned their first glimpse of the realities of war. The Japanese forces prepared to fend off their first air attack from the sea, but the Japanese public was kept in the dark.

The results of the raid bear out most convincingly the soundness of Admiral Halsey's decision. Doolittle accomplished his mission; the security of Halsey's forces, rather weak at best, remained intact, and the Japanese warlords were shown beyond question that their homeland was vulnerable. As a result, the

Japanese subsequently retained a greater number of forces in their homeland for defense. It is generally well accepted that the Doolittle raid had a marked psychological impact on both home fronts. The small striking force of American aircraft scared the daylights out of the Japanese military after 2,600 years of immunity, and these daring offensive Air Corps pilots, led by Jimmy Doolittle and sponsored by "Bull" Halsey, gave our people a much needed offensive shot in the arm. There was, however, a regrettable loss of aircraft and pilots to the Doolittle force. This must be analyzed relative to the probable losses to the Task Force which represented a good portion of the carrier strength in our Navy at that time. A valid evaluation of the soundness of the decision must correlate the point of view of Doolittle, the Air Commander, and that of Halsey, the over-all Task Force Commander. There has been little argument on this operation and it is rather doubtful that much will ensue. It is felt that one can state unequivocally that the decision made was sound. Halsey had struck again! The Japanese were to feel the sting of his deception and decisive blows again and again until the last minutes of the war in the Pacific.

The Battle of Midway—June 4, 1942

Midway is generally accepted as the turning point of the war in the Pacific, and most students of naval warfare agree it was the most significant action of the entire war. Admiral Spruance's Force was justifiably proud when it steamed into Pearl Harbor with swabs flying high at the *Enterprise* fore truck, a symbol of victory after the historic naval battle. But at the time, even amid the elation, the full import of the victory was not completely recognized by most of its participants.

Midway was a fascinating battle—militarily it has everything! The more one studies and contemplates the action of this battle, the more fascinating it becomes. It is one of the great sagas of the sea and naval warfare; it is a battle replete with heroism, devotion to duty, death and destruction, suspense and surprise. All of the problem areas of naval warfare seem inextricably woven into the story of this great naval air battle. At the battle of Midway all of the principles of war were either exploited or mishandled by the commanders on one side or the other. Problems of command, the contact, the weather, the objective, surprise, and security unfold to the student of naval tactics. We who were afforded the opportunity to live through this exciting battle will probably concede that this was the greatest of the entire war.

Aboard the *Enterprise* during the action at Midway, three particular aspects of the battle appeared to be decisive factors in its outcome. First: by exploitation of superb intelligence, the Commander in Chief of the Pacific Fleet was able to effect remarkable strategic concentration of far-flung forces; his tactical commanders were able to achieve surprise and defeat a markedly superior naval force. The pre-battle intelligence available to U.S. commanders at Midway was probably the best ever enjoyed in the history of naval warfare.

Second: the key tactical decision at Midway wasn't made by either Admiral Spruance or Admiral Fletcher. Commander Wade McClusky, the Air Group Commander of the *Enterprise*, made the most momentous decision in the entire engagement. Were it not for his decision to search for the Japanese Fleet when he failed to establish contact at their reported position, quite probably, in spite of the excellent intelligence, the battle would not have been won. The position reported from the initial PBY contact on the Japanese striking force was a point in latitude and longitude to the northwest of Midway Island. The contact also provided amplifying information that the Japanese Fleet was steaming on a southeasterly course at twenty-five knots to close Midway for initial attacks. There were diverse manners in which this initial contact was treated by the U.S. aircraft which were in the air at the time. Some ignored the course factor; McClusky did not. The *Enterprise* air group proceeded to the point where the Japanese were expected to be. But the enemy fleet was not there. Additional information from the PBY search planes was not forthcoming. Had the Japanese exceeded their twenty-five knot estimated speed? Had they turned around? Or had they commenced a retirement to the westward? These are the questions with which McClusky was obliged to wrestle in order to determine his course of action. A glimpse at his fuel gauge was not reassuring; he was being extended beyond a comfortable range. As a matter of fact he had been thrust into a situation that was in all respects anything but comfortable. There were some who emphasized the importance of low fuel, jettisoned bombs, and retreated to Midway. McClusky could have done so with justification, but he was determined to find the Japanese and attack. He decided that the Japanese had turned around, and he must seek them to the northwest. Thank God for Wade McClusky. Many of us would not be alive today were it not for the soundness of his decision. His judgment, determination, and courage in the development of the initial contact and subsequent attack on the *Kaga*, *Akagi*, and *Soryu* saved the day.

A third point flows logically from the McClusky action in the air incident: the Battle of Midway emphasized the importance of timing in tactical situations.

Perhaps it is not too widely known that prior to the time the *Enterprise* Air Group Commander was able to find and attack the enemy, a plain language contact report from one of the aircraft from the heavy cruiser *Tone* was heard on the big "E." This plane was reporting our position and the composition of our force. Fortunately the Commander of the Japanese striking fleet requested a verification of this report which must have seemed inconceivable to him as no U.S. carriers were to be available to oppose the occupation of Midway. Had not naval intelligence at Imperial Headquarters accounted for the *Saratoga* on the West Coast, the *Yorktown* heavily damaged in the Coral Sea, the *Lexington* sunk in the same battle? Was not Halsey sighted off Efate en route to the Coral Sea with the *Enterprise* and *Hornet*? This must be a mistake! *Machigai Naku* (no fooling)! Fortunately these Japanese cruiser scouting planes were rather vulnerable and this search aircraft was shot down just as the pilot began to repeat his contact. This episode must have caused some consternation in the minds of the Japanese.

But the fortunes of war or so-called breaks, good and bad, in the conduct of war, never are entirely one-sided. The periods of decision are filled with tension for both adversaries. Perhaps herein lies the foundation of the drama of our Admiral's decisions in their environmental setting of their wartime formations at sea. The Battle of Midway provides illustration of this truism. Like the Japanese, we had our troubles in dealing with the unknown: uncertainty as to how much of the enemy force was poised to strike, what degree of the information in the *Tone* plane report had been received by the Japs, and which of us would get there "fustest with the mostest." Understandably, whether Spruance, Slonim, or seaman, we all had that sinking feeling in the pits of our stomachs prompted by fear that the Japanese with their superior forces, in fact in the driver's seat, were about to provide us with the treatment we had hoped to administer to them. The feeling was one of relief and exhaustion when we learned that the *Enterprise* and *Yorktown* Air Groups were conducting their first attacks. The margin regarding time and force had been anything but conducive to equanimity. The maiden of good fortune had smiled most co-operatively at Admiral Spruance that morning.

We were relative neophytes in the sport of naval air warfare. Mistakes were made and lessons learned the hard way. What was Admiral Spruance's principal decision at Midway? He was forced to decide whether to turn west to rout the enemy fleet after their carriers had been sunk, or to steam eastward to avoid being forced into a night surface engagement. There has been much controversy around this decision to steam eastward rather than to the west where the enemy was located. In this matter, clarification has been gained by consideration of the threat posed by a night encounter of our cruisers with Yamamoto's battleships. This was a factor which properly weighed heavily on Admiral Spruance's mind, since such an encounter could well have proved disastrous. The facts available subsequent to this battle have confirmed the soundness of this decision.

We found that Point Option, now called PIM, also proved troublesome. A carrier force of limited strength, operating aircraft continuously, cannot maintain any direction other than into the wind, but this fact was somehow not apparent prior to the battle. This was an important principle learned.

Seniority has had a habit of frequently rearing its ugly head to impact upon command in the decisive actions, battles, and operations of war. Personalities have forced their way into areas of command in military operations throughout history.

Fate paved the way for Admiral Spruance to command the operation in a rather strange and not entirely acceptable manner. The *Yorktown* was put out of action very early in the game and consequently Admiral Fletcher shifted to the *Astoria* with the *Yorktown* survivors, relinquishing command to Admiral

Spruance. With respect to this command relationship problem, it is a curious point of speculation whether or not we would have lost the *Yorktown* and whether the ultimate outcome of the battle would have altered if the three carriers had operated as one formation under one commander.

Midway paved the way for victory in the Pacific. But, it also was the inception of the greatness of Admiral Raymond Spruance. Fortune smiled upon him again many times as our war progressed westward, but he always beckoned her with sound judgment and his uncanny ability to be one thought ahead of his adversary. Rear Admiral Burton B. Biggs, USN, termed him the luckiest white man alive. This was true, but Midway gave evidence that he was to become the greatest tactician in the history of our Navy. The soundness of Spruance's decisions will stand up to the scrutiny of posterity. His leadership and stature will provide nourishment to future greats through his example of objectivity and sensitivity and brilliant courage in action. Here was a leader who never made a mistake. He liked to think things through; and this he did.

The Turkey Shoot—June 20, 1944

Not too dissimilar to the Battle of Midway is the first Philippine Sea action, the so-called "Turkey Shoot." It is an extremely interesting operation in several respects. The most significant decision is, of course, Admiral Spruance's decision not to turn to the westward the night before the actual engagement occurred. This has been the subject of much discussion and controversy over a considerable period.

There is an interesting prelude to this operation. Admiral King had reviewed the overall plans for the Saipan Operation and was somewhat concerned over the fact that the voluminous amphibious plan weighed about seven pounds, whereas the fleet action annex to the Fifth Fleet Operation Plan was alarmingly light. He sent a dispatch to Admiral Nimitz asking him whether he felt that sufficient consideration had been given to the possibility of the enemy's coming out with his fleet to oppose the landings at Saipan. Admiral Nimitz assured him that both he and Admiral Spruance had discussed this at considerable length, with the *hope* that the Japanese fleet would come out. They were fully prepared to engage them should they sortie in defense of Saipan. In retrospect, it seems that neither felt, however, that it was highly probable.

Admiral King's visit to Saipan after the position had been secured, perhaps with a bit of fire in his eye, appears to have been significant. The purpose of his trip, quite reasonably, was to evaluate this decision. He probably wanted to obtain the facts that were available on the spot, to the people who were on the spot! The apparent approval by COMINCH of the conduct of the over-all amphibious operation and fleet action and the basic decisions was reassuring; it tended to confirm the soundness of the "Turkey Shoot" thinking.

Let us reconsider for a moment the basic decision involved: whether to turn westward to chase the enemy fleet after the coast watchers reported the Japanese fleet was steaming through San Bernadino Strait. It would perhaps appear that the key to the operation was based on Japanese plans for a free ride on the "merry-go-round." By means of utilizing the air fields on Guam for refueling, the range for Japanese based planes could be increased while remaining outside of effective striking range of our carriers. This they attempted to do.

Based on the relative composition and strength of the opposing forces, it did not seem probable that the Japanese were prepared to meet our Fleet in a frontal attack to contest our occupation of Saipan, even though the seizure of Saipan did pose a serious threat to the Empire. This assumption could be wrong, however, inasmuch as the Japanese fleet actually did come out in the Leyte operation for what practically amounted to a suicide "Banzai" attack on our fleet in order to deny the Philippines. However, it seems that the Japanese were more concerned about the Leyte operation, as there was a realization in the high command that the loss of the Philippines was the last stage in the strangulation of Japanese sea power and their ability to feed and sustain their nation. For the loss of the Philippines to the Japanese meant that their last line of sea communications would be ruptured and irreparable. Therefore, quite understandably, while the anticipated loss of Saipan was assessed as great, there is little question that the Japanese people did not become as frantic as they did later in the Leyte Gulf operation. This appears to be an extremely important factor. If the fleet were not moving in for a normal fleet action, a move to countermarch our forces would have resulted in no engagement whatsoever. We might have lost the opportunity to sink the important carriers *Shokaku* and *Taiho* and inflict other damage during the operation.

Based on the coast watchers' initial report of the Japanese fleet transiting San Bernadino Strait, Admiral Mitscher recommended to Admiral Spruance during the night that we head westward and attempt to engage the Japanese fleet at daylight. At approximately this same time the *Indianapolis* picked up a message from the *Zuikaku* which had been originated by the Commanding Officer of the *Shokaku*. We knew that in Japanese procedure the call sign of a commander in parenthesis meant the commander had originated the message and was at the station sending.

The *Shokaku* skipper's message was very brief. You could sense that it was being handled as a pretty hot potato and had the highest priority use in Japanese naval traffic. We were unable to read the message. However, we realized that it carried extreme urgency and that it was unusual in the sense that one carrier commander was sending it from another carrier. We considered the message as being of more tactical significance than the report of a conference aboard the sister ship. We evaluated it as a possible result of the sinking of the *Shokaku*, although we had no report to confirm this. As it had happened Captain Kossler in the *Cavalla* actually had put several torpedoes into and actually had sunk the *Shokaku* at the time reported in the message, but because he was being "held down" by ASW forces of the screen he was unable to report the results of the attack, and more importantly, he could not report the position of the Japanese fleet. At the time Admiral Mitscher's recommendation came in, we on the Staff were attempting to sell the idea of turning around; when Admiral Spruance completed his analysis of the situation, we realized we were wrong. Consequently, it would seem logical that there was no error in the Admiral's reasoning, concluding to remain in a position where he could provide adequate protection to the amphibious force at Saipan. *This was the basic objective of the operation.* As a matter of interest, many a verbal battle has been fought on this point through the years. By turning to the westward, Admiral Spruance anticipated an "end run" by the Japanese and wanted to be in a position to counter any thrust made at our amphibious forces. To have not remained in the vicinity of Saipan, he felt, would lay Turner's forces open to destruction, and he would be unable to prevent this. A salient point is that at this time our forces were being shadowed; we had constant and continual intercepts and radar confirmation of enemy aircraft which were in contact with our forces. There was no doubt that our every move was being reported almost instantaneously. On the other hand, we had no definite information revealing the exact location of the Japanese fleet, beyond that of the coast watchers—generally the least reliable source, professionally speaking. There was a misfortune in that one of our seaplanes operating out of Saipan "on a shoe-string" had contacted the enemy, but as a result of a communication failure this message was not received until about nine hours later. Had we known specifically the precise and continuous location of the enemy fleet, a turn to the west might well have been advisable. But because the Japanese were continuously aware of our location and because their plans probably had been developed on the basis of utilizing Guam to safely attack our forces with their carrier based aircraft, it seems that should we have turned to the westward that night, the Japanese would have countermarched in a similar direction. Once out of range for effectively using Guam's airfields for planned shuttle bombing, in all probability they would have retired. In this event we would never have been afforded an opportunity to destroy the forces which we were able to reach and attack during the operation.

Basically it seems that no mistakes were made in the major decisions of the "Turkey Shoot." However, there may have been one area in which we could have acted more effectively subsequent to our initial attacks. Our air attacks were of course made at extreme ranges and on their return many of our planes were forced to land in the water after running out of gasoline. There was considerable chaos in the Fleet that night. In one instance two planes landed aboard a carrier simultaneously; others in large groups reported they probably would not be able to get aboard since gas was running low. After recovering what aircraft we were able to land, the OTC [officer in tactical command] slowed from twenty-three to sixteen knots. The radical and vociferous element of the Staff argued for several hours that our best action at the time would be to maintain maximum sustained speed westward in order to exploit our force advantage in the morning by launching a dawn attack. We had less than ten hours till daylight; and at that time it was argued that actually the difference in distance would be only a matter of approximately fifty or sixty miles. We sensed that this range differential might be significant in dealing with "healthy ships" capable of retirement at high speeds. We urged that, as a search and rescue Task Group, we detach one CVL and all destroyers that were running low on fuel (and as usual after an air engagement there were many). But we argued (a frequent ingredient of tactical decisions) and urged that our main force must maintain maximum speed throughout the night. We discussed this approach with Vice Admiral J. S. McCain, later to become famous as Commander Task Force 38, who was riding aboard the *Indianapolis* as an observer during this operation. He agreed with our suggestions. The necessity for maintaining our speed was confirmed the next day when the first search plane to contact the enemy, a *Hancock* plane, reported his position and we plotted it as three hundred miles from our fleet center. An attack group was ordered to prepare for attacks immediately. Since the loss of aircraft had been very heavy the night before, the group was given specific orders to attack the force reported by this *Hancock* plane, but within a limitation of three hundred miles, considered to be the extreme range. As luck would have it, the THF pilot launched from the *Hancock* checked his navigation and discovered he had been mistaken in reporting the distance. It was not three hundred miles, but three hundred fifty, and consequently no attacks were launched on the second day.

The "Turkey Shoot" highlights the importance in naval warfare of evaluating the importance in naval warfare of evaluating principal objective. In addition, the battle again illustrates the importance of contact reports; problems involving erroneous or incomplete contact reports plagued our admirals at sea in making tactical decisions throughout almost the entire war.

Conclusions

This narrative of observations of naval command decisions raises the question as to what these observations can contribute to a more complete understanding of the common denominators of an effective exercise of command. In summary, the Marcus Raid highlights the importance of determination, courage, and the willingness to accept risks. The Doolittle Strike emphasizes the necessity of compromise followed by decisive action, and the need for flexibility in adjusting decisions to changing circumstances. In the Battle of Midway the elements of surprise, timing, and exploitation of good intelligence become salient factors. The first Philippine Sea Action, known as the "Turkey Shoot," stresses the need for proper evaluation of the principal objective, and the need for accurate planning.

Each operation discussed presents different segments of naval command decisions, which join to form a composite picture. As a result, it seems safe to conclude that the sound decision is composed of the following factors:

(1) good planning,

(2) good intelligence, and in addition a feel of the enemy, or sixth sense, to compensate for lack of intelligence which is always existent to a greater or lesser degree,

(3) good communications,

(4) good staff work,

(5) effective command relationships,

(6) a receptiveness to ideas and a willingness to compromise, imagination and an abundant supply of courage.

These are the elements of the sound decision, but to be sure, much more is involved. A sound decision is a product of the integrated action of a man in command of a situation, a situation which he has properly grasped through the intelligence provided by others, and to which he has applied his own reason and intuition. Inherent in this situation, to which he has reacted, and reacted properly, is a tremendous burden of responsibility and a demand for great courage. This is a fact which must not be minimized.

Basically, these points add up to the concluding thought that our ability to exploit sea power in an attainment of national objectives will continue to rest primarily on the soundness of the decisions made by naval commanders at the point of contact with the enemy.

10 "THE FUNCTIONS OF COMMAND"

CDR A. E. True, USN

Shortly after World War II had begun for the United States, this article appeared in *Proceedings* extolling the importance of action as an element of command. The timely appearance of this article can be seen in Commander True's discussion that contrasts command in the different venues of war and peace. Although admitting that "administration is a necessary evil," he observes that "during times of peace, when action is only simulated, or is unopposed by an actual enemy, there has been a tendency for administration functions to receive an undue and continuing importance." In contrast, he emphasizes that in wartime, "command is preparation for action, command leads to action, and command is action." With an air of slight sarcasm that is nonetheless relevant, he contends that "rushing through passages rattling papers is not action."

Acknowledging that in modern warfare commanders must make effective use of both men and machines, he divides the functions of command under the two broad headings of material and personnel, and then embraces many subsets, including strategy, tactics, and leadership. The end result is a useful blueprint for successful command.

"THE FUNCTIONS OF COMMAND"

By CDR A. E. True, USN, U.S. Naval Institute *Proceedings* (May 1942): 677–81.

> When Demosthenes was asked what was the first part of oratory,
> he answered "Action"; and which was the second, he replied "Action";
> and which was the third, he still answered "Action."—Plutarch

If Demosthenes could define the three parts of oratory with the one word, "Action," it seems even more appropriate that we define the functions of command by the same word, "Action." If we wish to be more specific and to include the lesser parts in the definition and discussion, the outline may be further expanded. The purpose of this article is to invite attention to the fact that the lesser parts actually are lesser parts and should be less emphasized; that the importance of the functions of command vary directly in the ratio in which they lead to action.

For the purpose in hand, the word "Command" is considered particularly to mean the command of a naval vessel, but it is believed that the discussion will apply equally well to command of a division, a squadron, a fleet, a company of infantry, or a turret crew. The fundamental purpose of the command is *action* by which a job is to be done or an enemy is to be destroyed. All other purposes and functions must be subordinate to, and contributory to, that purpose or they are valueless; probably worse than valueless. During long periods of peace, there is a natural tendency to place more emphasis on those functions of command which are most exercised in peace, i.e., upkeep and administration. When there is no action against an enemy, it is difficult to elevate the functions which directly support action to their proper relative importance. To be proficient in command, the individual must be able to perform *all* the functions of command, but at the same time he must never lose sight of the fundamental purpose of the command. He must stress those functions in the order in which they lead to effective action.

In modern warfare, on an increasing scale, men fight with machines. The commander must understand and make effective use of both men and machines. It is therefore logical to divide the functions of command into two major divisions, material and personnel. To add clarity to this discussion, the following is offered as an outline:

FUNCTIONS OF COMMAND
(A) *Material*
  (1) Upkeep
      (*a*) Inspection and repair
      (*b*) Logistics
  (2) Operation
      (*a*) Strategy
      (*b*) Tactics

(B) *Personnel*
  (1) Administration
      (*a*) Organization
      (*b*) Operation
  (2) Training
      (*a*) For upkeep
      (*b*) For operation
  (3) Operation or leadership
      (*a*) Initiative
          1. Speed
          2. Action
      (*b*) Morale
          1. Psychology
          2. Confidence
      (*c*) Judgment
          1. Logic
          2. Experience

Material consists of the tools with which we fight. Since the days when ships were merely floating platforms to carry sea soldiers into contact, material has grown increasingly important. It has also grown increasingly complicated. It is now necessary that many officers and men become technical specialists in order to keep this material in serviceable condition.

There is no desire to minimize its importance. It is only necessary to bear in mind that it is the use of tools rather than their upkeep that is the primary function of command. In times of peace, the tools are there, tangible and concrete, while action is in the intangible and uncertain future. It is natural that the commander should tend to concentrate his attention and his energy upon the perfection of his weapons. This course is not wrong so long as it does not usurp the place of preparation for action. Inspection and repair of material is an important but subsidiary function of command.

The operation of material *is* action. It is here that the commander can demonstrate his mastery of his tools. The swordsman may have a blade of the finest steel, but still his success will depend more upon his skill as a swordsman. The commander's weapon is his ship. He must know its strength and its weakness, its capabilities and its defects; above all he must know how to make the maximum use of its strength and capabilities. The knowledge that his point is sharp but that his steel is brittle is not enough unless he uses the weapon in such a manner as to take advantage of the sharpness of the point while he maneuvers to guard the brittle steel. When war is upon us, we must fight with what we have. It is usually the unskilled swordsman who lays his defeat to the faulty blade.

The operation of a ship as a weapon may be divided into two phases. The preparation of the weapon for action and its proper placing may be called strategy. The actual conduct of the action may be called tactics. Each requires a complete understanding of the weapon, and a skill in its use, on the part of the commander. This must be a personal understanding and a personal skill. No amount of leadership, or personality, or even morale can take its place. The commander must get the most from his ship as a good jockey gets the most from his horse. One might say that good strategy depends upon understanding of the weapon; that good tactics depends upon the skill in handling it. Strategical action should be based upon preliminary study, logical reasoning, and careful planning. Tactical action should be based upon training, experience, and practice.

The second major division of the functions of command is personnel, under which may be listed the functions of administration, training, and operation or leadership. It is here that the commander must possess an ability that is different and distinct from his technical skill in ship-handling and his use of inanimate material. Our personnel are basically and fundamentally the best in the world. This is so because they have developed under a democratic government as educated, free, thinking individuals. They have a foundation of courage, intelligence, and initiative. For this very reason the task of adequate leadership is more difficult and requires more ability than would be the case with men who have not grown up in an atmosphere of freedom and individualism. The leader must be able to command loyalty by virtue of ability, honesty, and integrity of character. Intelligent men are quick to sense the existence or lack of existence of these. The inferior leader may ride along on the basic loyalty of his men to the greater issues of cause and country, but he himself is a liability rather than an asset.

Administration covers the details of organization and operation for the performance of any required function. Any body of men must be organized to produce effective and coordinated action. A good organization is a basic and fundamental necessity. It consists of the selection and assignment of appropriate parts of the general task to such personnel as are best fitted to perform them. Since there are many different types of tasks which a naval command must be prepared to perform, its organization is necessarily somewhat complicated. The essential elements are: (1) That no part of any probable task shall be overlooked or left unassigned; (2) that the maximum use be made of the available man power. It is in the second essential that naval organizations are most frequently at fault. Due to the difficulty of duplicating given war conditions in peace time, a tendency has grown up to be wasteful of man power. The personnel organization must cover such a multitude of possible tasks, under varying conditions, that it is necessary that it be flexible. It is the province of the commander then to adapt it to the varying tasks and conditions as they occur. The better the original organization, the less administration will be necessary in operation. The less administration intrudes itself into operation, the more effective will be the action. Administration then should be an important but preliminary function of command. It should be practically ended before action commences. During times of peace, when action is only simulated, or is unopposed by an actual enemy, there has been a tendency for administration functions to receive an undue and continuing importance. It is exemplified by the so-called commander who buries himself industriously in a stack of papers and labors under the delusion that he is promoting efficiency and action, when in reality he is a clerk. The reports receive too much attention; the action receives too little.

Training of personnel is the preparation for action in time of peace; it naturally becomes the primary function of command because it is the substitute for action. It must accomplish an understanding of, and familiarity with, the tools to be used in action; the care and preservation of those tools; and the operation or use of the tools. The first two of the foregoing are principally a part of education; the third is principally a matter of practice. The time element in modern warfare is all important. The man and machine, the man and his weapon, must be made as one with understanding and mastery. Perfection in use and operation of the weapon is attained by continuous practice and experience. Each man must achieve a skill in the performance of his operation, no matter how small nor how simple the operation is, so that not one second of time is lost, nor one movement wasted. Each man bears to his individual task the same relation that the commander bears to the unit as a whole. The commander has trained his men when the correct action and the spontaneous natural impulse, both in himself and in his men, is one and the same.

The last and most important function of command is personal leadership in action. In a military service, this can only meet its ultimate test when there is action, i.e., in war. No amount of technical skill, no amount of administrative ability can compensate for lack of it. Its component parts are initiative, morale, and judgment.

Initiative is a primary requisite to leadership and to action. It is that state of mind which tends to grasp the essentials of a given situation quickly, to determine what action is required, and to undertake that action promptly. To some individuals initiative is a natural quality. They are those often characterized as "born leaders." The quality may, however, be developed by practice, or it may be suppressed. The commander must develop his own initiative at every opportunity. If he purposely searches every situation that presents itself, whether important or inconsequential, selects the appropriate course of action, and promptly pursues it with energy, he will eventually reach that state when his reaction to any situation will be a natural and spontaneous impulse to action. It is equally important that he encourage this quality in his subordinates. No human being, however capable, can personally direct every detail of action in the manifold situations that arise in war. It is another weakness of peace-time training that so many commanders attempt to supervise personally and direct action in every detail when the stress of war is not upon them. They thus deny and suppress all initiative in their subordinates. They are not only failing to train their subordinates properly but they are actively preventing them from training themselves. Peace-time communications have been too good. When battle is joined, these same commanders will see failure because their subordinates stand aloof and wait for orders. Initiative is necessary in all echelons. It is not, however, the only requirement for leadership. The "born leader" is not necessarily a good leader. Initiative must be supplemented by good morale and good judgment.

Morale is one of the chief responsibilities of command. Napoleon has said that "The moral is to the physical as three to one" and this estimate may not be dismissed lightly. History is replete with records of victories of inferior forces by reason of superior morale. Morale is based on two principal factors: first, the understanding of his subordinates by the leader; second, the confidence of the subordinates in their leader. The best morale is not possible without both. Every individual and every group of men present a specific and unique problem in psychology. The greater the education and intelligence of a group, the greater is the problem of their psychological handling. Intelligent men must be led rather than driven. They tend to ask why. This does not mean that the commander must broadcast secret information which his subordinates do not need to know. It does mean that they must understand what they are trying to do and why. It means that they must be instilled with a desire to co-operate with, and to assist the commander in the accomplishment of his objective. Subordinates must have an objective in order that they may use their intelligence and initiative in coordinating their common efforts to a common end. If it be otherwise, man power, will power, and brains will be wasted. Confidence in the commander is a prerequisite to intelligent co-operation and to wholehearted support by subordinates. To attain this, it is of course desirable that the leader be more capable, more efficient, more courageous, and more intelligent than any of his juniors. Unfortunately, in any large organization, this cannot always be the case. The solution is not to attempt to deceive the subordinates by a pretension to these qualities. Intelligent men are very quick to penetrate such attempted deception and the result is the loss rather than the gain of confidence. The proper solution is complete honesty, courage, loyalty, and integrity on the part of the commander. It must be borne in mind that men do not face death for thirty dollars a month. They are ready and anxious to give their loyalty if that loyalty is deserved and accepted. With it they are ready to give their ability, courage, initiative, and intelligence to the commander who is wise enough to make use of what is freely his. If he does make use of it, he will have the confidence of his crew.

Judgment has two principal bases—logic and experience. Logic alone may be trusted as a guide in an exact science but war is an art rather than an exact science. Logic, in war, should therefore be tempered and guided by experience. Experience alone is a poor guide because it rejects the new and untried merely because it is new and untried. The commander who is young will frequently depend too heavily upon his theories and his reasoning, and tend to neglect the lessons of experience. The older commander, on the other hand, often gives undue weight to traditional methods and is reluctant to try the new. Age, in itself, however, is not always a true indicator. Napoleon, for instance, gained experience at an early age both from his own actions and from those of others. At the same time, some individuals are able to keep their minds young enough to apply logic to their rich store of experience at very advanced ages. These are, perhaps, the best and the wisest commanders of all, but unfortunately they are rare. The essential point is that the successful commander must be able to attain that delicate balance between logic and experience in order to develop his judgment to the fullest. Every action must be preceded by judgment and decision. Upon the accuracy of that judgment may depend the lives of many men, or the fortunes of a country. Judgment, therefore, must be not only good but the best.

To summarize, briefly, command is preparation for action, command leads to action, and command is action. The minor functions must be given a minor place. Administration is a necessary evil, the less the better. Rushing through passages rattling papers is not action. Upkeep of material and training of personnel are important prerequisites to successful action and are therefore important functions of command. Operation of material and leadership of personnel are of the essence of action and are therefore the most important functions of command.

11 "A SEA STORY NOT EASILY TOLD"

LCDR Thomas J. Cutler, USN (Ret.)

Although with the passage of time I am unable to verify this, I was once told by a commander attending prospective commanding officer's school that this article was being used as part of the curriculum there. I have also received enough positive feedback over the years that I will risk possible accusations of a lack of hubris on my part and include it in this anthology, hoping that it will have the desired effect of providing food for thought toward a greater good. Sins are often better described by the repentant sinner than by the preacher on the pulpit.

"A SEA STORY NOT EASILY TOLD"

By LCDR Thomas J. Cutler, USN (Ret.), U.S. Naval Institute *Proceedings* (August 1996): 8-10.

What follows is not easily told. I have not shared this "sea story" even with my wife until now.

One evening, at twilight, I had assumed the watch as officer of the deck (OOD) of a destroyer on routine operations in the midst of a fleet exercise. Shortly after taking the deck, my attention was focused on a nearby frigate that was part of the same exercise. I honestly do not remember the exact circumstances that led to what happened next, but the bottom line was that I made an error in assessing what was happening—the frigate was launching or recovering a helicopter and I misread the lights and her intentions such that I allowed our two ships to come dangerously close to one another. The captain was not on the bridge at the time, and the incident occurred so quickly that there was not time to call him before it was over.

Within minutes, a signal light on the frigate began blinking its angry eye at me, and soon my duty signalman was handing me a message from the captain of the frigate. It was from captain to captain and said something to the effect of "Please don't do that again; I have enough gray hairs."

My captain was an extremely competent individual who was one of the best shiphandlers I have ever known. He was a demanding—almost formidable—leader, who wore the Navy and Marine Corps medal for heroism, earned while helping to save lives in the aftermath of a major collision at sea. It was this latter fact that also made him an extremely cautious captain when it came to placing trust in his officers of the deck. The collision he had lived through was one of the worst in U.S. Navy history, and the blame ultimately had been placed on the OOD of the ship my captain had been serving in. Through most of my tour in his destroyer, there were only three qualified OODs. One of the department heads nearly had his career ruined because our captain never did permit him to qualify. Needless to say, we who had qualified were not anxious to do anything to subvert the captain's trust in us.

When the signalman—a senior petty officer in my department—brought the message to me, I read it as one might read one's own death warrant. After several moments of careful deliberation, I handed the signal back and said, "How about losing this for me? I'll take the responsibility if anything comes of it, but I don't want the Captain to see this." (Twenty years later, this still is very difficult to put on paper.) The signalman crumpled the message, threw it over the side, and returned to the bridge. I was both relieved and heartsick.

Some weeks after the incident—weeks spend in dread that my captain and the commanding officer of the frigate might splice the mainbrace together in the O-Club—we were involved in a graded towing exercise in which we were to take turns with a cruiser towing one another. It was part of an intensive fleet training workshop and we were under some pressure to get through the training and to do well so that we would be ready for an impending deployment. After a thorough briefing, during which the Fleet Training Group personnel emphasized the need for very cautious acceleration while effecting the tow, we began towing the cruiser. The captain had the conn and was in sound-powered communication with the executive officer (XO), who was on the fantail.

For reasons I no longer can recall, we got off to a slow start on the exercise, and because the day was growing short, the captain's patience began to wane. Anxious to complete the exercise, he began to rush things a bit and was accelerating too quickly as he began the tow. The XO called from the fantail, warning the captain that he was straining the hawser. The OOD warned the captain that he felt we were going too fast. The captain ignored both warnings and persisted until we heard what sounded like a rifle shot as the hawser parted.

Minutes later, the captain handed the duty signalman a message addressed to the captain of the cruiser and the officer in charge of the Fleet Training Group contingent. In it, the captain blamed the incident on a faulty hawser. He later filed an official report up the chain of command repeating the faulty hawser excuse.

Within a few weeks, two naval officers serving in the same ship had compromised their integrity to save themselves embarrassment and possible damage to their careers. The signalmen who helped me with my crime surely must have thought less of me after that night when I asked him to ignore his duty and toss an official Navy communication into the sea. I know that we who served in the captain's wardroom thought less of him when we saw him write that message exonerating himself by claiming what we all knew was not true.

Why did we do this? Why did we compromise our honor in the face of adversity? Personal honor always has been among my highest ideals, and I have no doubt that the same was true for my captain. Yet both of us prostituted our integrity rather than admit we had made a mistake.

I am tempted to argue that I saw my entire naval career in jeopardy and that the Navy, next to my family and my nation, was and is the most important aspect of my life. I am tempted to assume that the captain was under great pressure to do well and that he too saw his error as more significant than perhaps it was. But both of us lost part of our souls when we decided to cover up our mistakes rather than admit them to our superiors.

It is possible that this captain and I are atypically poor examples of naval officers who never should have been commissioned and entrusted with leadership roles in the defense of our nation. My actions on that fateful watch so many years ago dictate that I can never dismiss this as a possibility in my case. But as a somewhat objective observer in the captain's case, I can say honestly that I do not believe this to be true.

If we were not morally corrupt individuals, why did we act as though we were? Perhaps the answer lies embedded in the problems that currently are plaguing the Naval Academy, where some midshipmen are known to have lied rather than admit to their mistakes. Perhaps there is a clue in the recent death of a Chief of Naval Operations who appears to have killed himself rather than admit he made a mistake.

Perhaps the answer can be found through a careful scrutiny of the code that we naval officers live by—or try to live by. From the earliest days of our training as naval officers—whether at the Naval Academy, Officer Candidate School, or in the Naval Reserve Officer Training Corps—we teach ourselves that perfection is the goal. We use terms like *can do* and *4.0* and *110%*. We emphasize the great achievements of this Navy we are privileged to serve, and those achievements—John Paul Jones's incredible victory off Flamborough Head, the upstart U.S. frigates defeating the powerful ships of the Royal Navy in the War of 1812, the two-ocean victory at sea in World War II—take on a mythical iconography that puts them into the realm of superhuman achievement. Such things are immensely inspiring and a source of great pride, but they also may set standards that cannot always be duplicated. And when real flesh-and-blood human beings, wearing the same blue and gold as these superheroes of our past, are not always able to achieve the perfection their heritage and training demands, there may be an undeserved sense of inadequacy or failure.

We must not, under any circumstance, turn our backs on our proud past, and we should not strive for anything less than perfection, but we must allow pragmatism to coexist with idealism. We must recognize that despite the tremendous achievements of John Paul Jones, Stephen Decatur, and Bull Halsey, these men also made mistakes. We must convey to aspiring young naval officers that perfection is the goal and accountability is a mandatory component of responsibility, but a willingness to admit error also is essential to sound leadership. We must continually remind ourselves that we and our fellow human beings—whether they are midshipmen, lieutenants, or CNOs—are not always going to be able to do the impossible, that sometimes a 3.8 or 90% is going to have to do. This does not mean that we accept perpetual mediocrity or that we forgive every sin. It does mean that we must weigh each transgression against intent, that we must convince ourselves and those who follow in our footsteps that making a mistake is not the ultimate sin but that cover-up is.

We have succeeded in inculcating in ourselves the pursuit of perfection. Now we must devote our efforts toward an equally effective pursuit of a realistic code of conduct that includes the requirement to admit our shortcomings. Our earliest training must place this requirement on an equal footing with loyalty and physical courage and ahead of our desire to be perfect. Perhaps our fitness reports can be modified to include a block for "ability to admit mistakes." Perhaps we need to indoctrinate ourselves with a list of commandments that include the following:

- I will strive for perfection in all that I do, to uphold the proud traditions of our naval service in every way.
- I will remember that my subordinates, my peers, my superiors, and I sometimes will fall short of perfection.
- I will never choose to hide my mistakes but will openly admit them so that I and others might learn from them.

That night when I tossed a message into the sea, it was not the first, nor the last, mistake I would make in my naval career. But it stands out because I chose to cover it up rather than take the honorable course. I suspect that I am not alone among naval officers suffering the pain that such decisions cause. If we are to uphold the proud heritage of the U.S. Navy, we must recognize that there is honor in admitting our shortcomings, and we must find the means to make that recognition paramount in our thoughts and in our actions.

12 "'GET OFF MY BACK, SIR!'"

CDR Robert E. Mumford Jr., USN

What follows is a useful discussion of one of the major issues concerning command. As mentioned in the introduction to this book, those having had command frequently complain that too often they receive too much interference from their superiors. Commander Mumford addresses this issue head-on with this article. What makes this article particularly noteworthy—and also serves as a testament to the value of the Naval Institute's open forum—is the amount of follow-on discussion that it provoked. Discussion continued for more than a year in the pages of *Proceedings* (included below) and ultimately led to a whole new article by another author (see next chapter).

Commander Mumford's ship was awarded the "Arleigh Burke Fleet Trophy" in 1975 while he was in command, and he wrote this article while heading the prospective commanding officer/prospective executive officer human resource training program at the Naval Amphibious School in Coronado, California.

"'GET OFF MY BACK, SIR!'"

By CDR Robert E. Mumford Jr., USN, U.S. Naval Institute *Proceedings* (August 1977): 18–23.

On the West Coast, a skipper is ordered to terminate his highly successful management incentive program because some of his men have completed their assigned tasks in less than the standard eight hour day and have been allowed to go on liberty. At an East Coast port, all command duty officers are required to be on the quarterdeck between 1600 and 2000 daily to ensure that the liberty party is in acceptable attire. In Washington, a Navy civilian employee is reprimanded for a security violation because she failed to sign off her safe at close of business, even though her safe was properly locked. What do these seemingly unrelated events have in common? Very simply, they illustrate the most pervasive and insidious management problem in the Navy today: the means/ends inversion, a focus on activity in lieu of goals. Procedures are stressed to the exclusion of substance.

There are many ways to describe The Problem, any one of which provides the flavor, but none of which seems to fully explain its extent. In traditional Navy jargon, excessive rudder orders are being issued, seniors telling juniors not only what they are expected to achieve, but *how* to reach that goal. Some management consultants would tell us that we have lost sight of our objectives; others call it micromanagement or "Big Brotherism."

It requires no special management background to recognize that we have a problem in the Navy. The very size of type commander regulations indicates that something is wrong. Exasperated skippers have suggested that John Paul Jones could not have defeated the *Serapis* if he had been burdened by so much paper. If one takes the time to go beyond the bulk of regulations and examine the substance, the full impact of The Problem becomes obvious. In every publication of regulations the author has examined, there are numerous examples of extremely detailed guidance. It is either so obvious as to be demeaning, or it establishes procedures that are unnecessary for accomplishing worthwhile goals.

These examples indicate that our people in command are not just being given goals to reach; rather, they are being told "how to" in great detail. One logically needs then to ask, "Is this really a problem?" Aren't military people *supposed* to do what they're told? Isn't this the way it has always been? Is the organization really being damaged by detailed guidance from above? If you want the answers that count most, go to the people on the cutting edge, fleet commanding and executive officers. They may express themselves in different words, but their consensus is clear: they feel overwhelmed and stifled by excessive direction. They are frustrated, angry, and depressed by the realization that what should be the most rewarding years of their lives—the professional peak of their careers—are not all that satisfying. Some have described themselves as puppets, being moved by strings from above. Having thought that they would be able to exercise their creative capacities, they find that they are being forced into doing things the way someone else thinks best. Instead of concentrating on combat readiness, skippers and execs are forced into meeting administrative checkoff lists and fitting themselves and their commands into a mold of standardized operation that is uncomfortable at best.

There have been many cases in recent years of top-performing officers refusing commands. Worse, some of those who took command admit in private that they would resign if they could do so gracefully. The Navy, shocked and dismayed by this, seems ready to believe that we have somehow bred a line of timid officers who want to shrink from responsibility. It is always more comforting to blame the individual than to accept the unhappy conclusion that something may be wrong with the organization. What is lacking is not acceptance of responsibility (in most officers), but rather the lack of an opportunity to be creative and independent.

More than just commanding officers are affected. Junior officers seem deeply troubled and turned off by The Problem. Many express their deep frustration and discouragement by exchanging the blue and gold for mufti at the first legal opportunity. It was not without good cause that one of the important initiatives of the early Seventies was to put "fun and zest" back into the system. In the author's judgment, that effort largely fell flat. It is a rare skipper who has not been told by a young division officer or a department head that he doesn't consider the prestige and power of command to be worth the "hassle." More often than not, the officers who express this thought are among the most talented and ambitious on board. We have created a gap between the image with which we recruit officers and the reality of their existence. The romantic image is of a man who goes to sea, leads other men, exercises discretion and power—an independent thinker and doer, an individual in an era of massive organizations. In reality, he is closer to a colorless cipher, conforming to countless paper requirements in order to survive.

We are developing a corps of officers who look for answers in publications but can't fight their own ships. They know how to conform but not create, interpret but not innovate. And we delude ourselves that this is sufficient. Because we have the peacetime capacity to control fleet units in the remote areas of the globe, we assume that these communications will be present during wartime. Thus, the qualities of independence, initiative, and judgment are no longer quite so important. We continue to pay lip service to these characteristics, but our actions belie our words. Our inspection and promotion systems reward those who precisely follow the methodology ordered from above. We seldom, if ever, measure results instead of procedures. In addition to hurting retention, adversely affecting officer development, and causing dissatisfaction, The Problem detracts from the achievement of the Navy's raison d'être: combat readiness. Behavioral scientists for years have reported that motivation is best achieved (after the basic needs have been met) by permitting people a good deal of latitude in their vocational environment. By participating in goal development and determining the course to reach those goals, "ownership" develops, and people have a personal stake in ensuring successful accomplishment. Indeed, one of the conceptual foundations of the Navy's own Human Resource Availability is increased commitment through development by the crew of unit goals and the steps to reach them. What the institution has blessed within units during one week of an 18-month cycle, however, is inconsistent with standard practices toward units during the entire cycle. An examination of fleet and type commander goals reveals a number of items which are oriented toward compliance with procedures rather than outcomes. Full use of training devices is an example.

Determining the cause for this devitalizing problem which permeates the entire organization is difficult at best. Undoubtedly, there is no single reason, but rather a cluster of norms, values, pressures, and constraints have contributed. There is no easy target to point to as scapegoat; it is all of us and none of us. While venting one's spleen against staff personnel may provide some measure of satisfaction and ameliorate temporarily the ill effects of a complaining ulcer, it does little to identify the real culprit(s). Some possible factors may be suggested.

Perhaps the largest factor contributing to The Problem is a downward spiraling phenomenon whose elements are failure, distrust, direction, and overload. The cycle typically begins with an acknowledged failure at some level. When a senior is put under excessive pressure by *his* senior, overreaction can occur, with the result that subordinates are no longer trusted to accomplish their jobs. Assuming that some will fail without guidance, the senior issues directives to prevent another disaster in the area in question. These are followed by inspections to ensure that the senior's program has been implemented and by command attention to preclude embarrassment. The more these programs are directed from above, the more an officer's time at the unit level is dominated by compliance with "how to's" and the less time is spent on achieving the goals themselves. Eventually, one's capacity for supervision becomes overloaded, an important item receives less attention than it warrants, another failure occurs, and the cycle is reinforced and repeated. The number of inspections and "assist" visits being imposed on our units suggests that we have reached criticality. Apparently, however, efforts are being made to reduce the number of such visits.

"Excessive staff echelons in the chain of command" is often identified as a major structural deficiency, and it may be one cause of The Problem. As directives depart each level, there is a tendency to interpret and provide policy guidance. Very often, this guidance includes added "how to's." What begins as a relatively simple objective at the four-star level may end at the unit level as a detailed plan of attack, completely foreclosing any opportunity for individual initiative. It is unreasonable to assume that it will be otherwise, without conscious effort. C. Northcote Parkinson, originator of the famous Parkinson's Laws, told us years ago that work expands to meet the time available. Thus, when staff positions are filled with energetic, bright officers, those officers are going to find something to do with their time. Directives follow directives, and commanders at each level feel it is necessary to issue implementing instructions. But paper alone proves neither loyalty nor effectiveness.

The necessity for a major change can result in The Problem. One example that comes to mind is the equal opportunity issue. While many thoughtful and dedicated people at all levels recognized that the Navy had major racial problems, insufficient progress was being made to satisfy ethical and legal demands. In the face of undesirable racial incidents, dramatic action was deemed necessary. The decision was made in Washington to require certain organizational changes in each unit, such as creation of the Minority Affairs Representative and the Human Relations Council. One can quibble endlessly whether these were necessary when a chain of command was functioning, but the point is that commanding officers were being told *how* to achieve a very admirable and essential goal. One result was that many officers still resent the program, despite being personally committed to equal opportunity and treatment.

In the author's opinion, a primary cause of The Problem is that—short of combat—we have trouble judging performance, despite 200 years of experience. For a variety of reasons, the surface community seems to have the most difficulty in this area. Our ships are seldom really evaluated against each other or by an objective minimum standard. And even our Battle Efficiency E competition involves a large measure of subjectivity. Because it is often easier to establish and monitor evaluative criteria around procedures than objectives, we rely on these factors to judge units. How are combat readiness, reliability, and casualty control measured? Who does the judging?

We know from past failure what doesn't work. For years there was competition between units which used certain exercises gleaned from *Ship Exercises* (FXP-3). But ships from the same squadron usually evaluated each other. Not unexpectedly, results were often compromised through mutual interests. A squadron commander could not be expected to be objective either. The more ships in his squadron that achieved departmental Es and other awards, the better he looked. When the author was a shipboard department head, he was the senior inspector for an amphibious battle problem on board a ship in the same squadron. The performance of the inspected ship was judged marginal (including a number of clear safety violations), but she received the annual amphibious assault award after the grades were elevated by the squadron commander. Self-evaluated exercises meet the needs of a training program, but they can hardly be used to determine the achievement of acceptable levels of performance. We have few measurable goals, and those that do exist, we often discount.

It appears that the Navy may be reluctant to accept the results of legitimate, objective competition. Humans in all walks of life believe that they can subjectively judge who is the best performer, yet that judgment often mirrors those who are the most liked. When a subordinate who is out of favor demonstrates success, the senior is often made very uncomfortable and surprised. He must then either reevaluate his assessment of the individual or downplay and ignore the performance. If the Navy as an institution is going to adopt objective criteria for evaluating officer performance, it must be willing to accept the results and reward the winner.

A seductive attraction of standardization can also be a contributing factor to The Problem. There appears to be a strong drive toward standardization in every large bureaucratic organization, irrespective of its function or composition. It does have its benefits and is sometimes necessary, but it is important to understand that standardization should not be a goal in itself. It protects the mediocre and incompetent to some degree and usually prevents gross errors. But it stifles the creative impulse of the most talented managers and precludes discovery of improved methods. Standardization is most beneficial when applied to technical problems but is often counter-productive in managing people.

What is the solution for The Problem? Just as there is no single cause, there is no one easy answer. An institution as large as our Navy cannot be changed overnight. When he was Chief of Naval Operations, Admiral Arleigh Burke reportedly bewailed the amount of energy required to alter the course of the organization by a single degree. There is an incredible amount of momentum accumulated in the habitual ways of conducting routine business, and the Navy has been deeply involved in the "how to" mode for many years. Old ways die particularly hard, and there will be powerful (and sincere) voices of dissent from many quarters if the Navy elects to change its *modus operandi*. It will be claimed that without detailed guidance, standards of "professional" excellence will not be met, and the readiness of the Navy will suffer, perhaps irreparably, while the "experiment" of concentrating on goals is conducted.

The above notwithstanding, improvement can be realized, and happily, without the necessity for change at the fleet level and above. Leaders at every level can make a conscious decision to get out of the "how to" business. Each can excise from his collection of directives those which contain rudder orders and refrain from getting back into the business with messages and suggestions. Individual people and commands within the Navy can adopt management by objectives, a technique where goals are mutually determined by superior and subordinate, and the subordinate is left to his own devices as to how to reach those goals. His fitness report would reflect how well the objectives were met. Management by objectives is not new to the Navy, and it has some strong advocates, but it often has been abandoned when difficulties have been encountered in implementation. While management by objectives is not the panacea for all Navy management problems, it certainly can contribute to eliminating the feelings of frustration experienced by so many commanding officers.

Of course, for objective-oriented management to be effective, there must be measurable goals. The Navy has developed meaningful objective criteria in some areas. It should continue to establish operational evaluations to determine who is meeting goals and who is falling short. Creating objective criteria and testing procedures is easy in some areas and difficult in others. There are already sufficient exercises and criteria for gunnery and aerial bombardment evaluation, but operations and communications testing is more formidable.

In order to achieve objectivity, special evaluation groups (not in the chain of command) should be established to judge performance. The Board of Inspection and Survey is an excellent example of an existing, no-nonsense, results-oriented evaluation group. Similar teams could be created to judge every facet of naval warfare. But this evaluation should be limited to outcomes, not whether records have been maintained, schools attended, or training programs conducted. Staffs in the chain of command should minimize their current roles of monitoring and evaluation and emphasize support and assistance to the operating forces. The fleet training groups should once and for all be restricted to training. The suggested evaluation groups should judge the final battle problem of a refresher training period. As it is, there is a conflict of interest between training and evaluation, for the judges are personnel from the organization which is charged with training. Complete objectivity does not always result.

One change that could be made overnight to provide commanding officers more latitude and authority would be to modify the restriction on days per quarter that ships can operate. The goal is clearly not to keep ships in port, but to conserve fuel and money. As it is, a ship could theoretically "cowboy" around the ocean for each of its allotted days, squandering fuel and exercising inefficient engineering practices without significant penalty. Why not allot to each ship an equitable amount of fuel and let the ship determine how it is to be expended? A ship with competent engineers, a motivated crew, and an innovative captain can probably figure ways of spending more training time at sea, thus meeting other combat readiness-related objectives.

Closely allied with the limit on days at sea per quarter is the wider problem of the entire quarterly employment schedule. There are usually four levels in the chain of command involved in establishing and changing schedules. The least influential is the ship herself. The number of personnel associated with this process is enormous, and the time and resources required, impressive. It is the author's belief that a simplified system, involving commanding officers to a greater degree, would result in conservation of effort at many levels. Rather than schedule in-port time, upkeep, individual exercises, and other very detailed forms of employment, a ship could be scheduled for COD—commanding officer's discretion. During that time, he could be under way, conducting maintenance, undergoing in-port training, or whatever he deemed appropriate. Imagine the energy that could be saved in not having to process every minor change in schedule. There are undoubtedly many other places in scheduling where a commanding officer can be given more latitude without disrupting the obvious necessity of coordinating and preplanning outside support activities associated with complex multi-unit exercises at sea and major maintenance ashore.

Another graphic example of an area where procedures have become more important than substance—and have eroded the commanding officer's discretion—is individual training. The Navy has implemented the Personnel Qualification Standard (PQS) system in every unit and for most ranks and rates. It is not merely recommended, but required, and many inspections now include the checking of PQS. PQS does, of course, have merit. The materials associated with the program have been developed at great cost and effort and often are of excellent quality. But the system requires considerable officer supervision and paperwork, and it does not necessarily achieve a goal. In today's cliché, what counts is the bottom line, and the bottom line in individual training is whether or not a man knows his job and can do it. If he doesn't, all the systems in use have failed. During inspections, what should be checked are not marks on a schedule but demonstrated knowledge. One unobtrusive measure which could be used would be to review average scores during the previous advancement exams. Another method would be random questioning of both officer and enlisted personnel. During ship visits, one Inspector General of the Navy asked men to demonstrate the use of an oxygen breathing apparatus, reasoning that if the men couldn't take the pressure of an admiral watching, they wouldn't be able to don the equipment in an emergency. As painful as such tests can be for a unit's supervisory personnel, they unequivocally measure results and cannot be "gundecked" by the saltiest operator. We need to eliminate most aspects of command and administrative inspections that deal with procedures and instead concentrate our limited examination time on the real elements of combat readiness.

A far more complicated and radical departure from current practices would be to restore more discretionary financial authority to the unit level. This is clearly a long-term venture which will require substantial in house planning and congressional approval. Yet it would free the commanding officer from the artificial constraints that now limit his ability to achieve readiness. Instead of funding food, fuel, spare parts, and salaries out of different pockets, a command could determine what element needed budgetary priority. There should be no reason why a skipper could not compensate a man who is doing the work of three petty officers (because of a Navy-wide shortage in a certain rating), nor utilize fuel money for spare parts, if that met a higher need. Commanding officers should be given the opportunity to retain funds in a "savings account" status past the fiscal year end. This would replace the current custom of a mad rush to expend funds during the last few weeks of the year. The present feast-or-famine atmosphere not only dictates against prudent fiscal practices at the unit level, it also regularly draws substantial unfavorable publicity to all the services.

What would be required to implement these changes would be nothing short of a major change in fiscal procedures, but this appears technically feasible. Indeed, Dr. Robert Anthony, Assistant Secretary of Defense (Financial Management) proposed a very similar concept a decade ago. The Navy did considerable research on the plan, nicknamed Project Prime, and attempted a shipboard pilot program. However, the effort proved unsuccessful, largely because of a lack of congressional support. Laws limiting discretion in the expenditure of public monies were neither repealed nor modified, and therefore new budgeting and obligating procedures could not be used, and the project was abandoned. Despite past problems, increased pressures on the armed services for improved management may now permit another attempt. Neither DoD nor Congress should object to modified budgeting if it can be demonstrated that the change would result in improved readiness. (Retention, quite clearly, is a major factor in the readiness equation.)

The above suggestions for reducing rudder orders in all their various forms by no means constitute an all-inclusive list. Valuable ideas for the establishment of a goal-oriented Navy will likely be triggered, however, in the minds of every officer with a modicum of fleet experience. Major change will come to the institution only when the cause for widespread dissatisfaction is recognized and accepted and the commitment is made to find a solution. The objective should be an environment of reasonable decentralization with clearly understood goals and priorities at every level. Diversity of styles and methods should be tolerated if not encouraged. Perhaps most importantly, occasional failures should be accepted as the price of developing initiative, innovation, and bold leadership. It should be a system where restraint is exercised in imposing procedures, where sophisticated communications are properly used as a tool instead of a means to tighten control. If this occurs, the Navy will once again be noted for its independent, resourceful seafaring captains, invigorated by modern leadership skills and strengthened by advanced technology. In short, to eliminate The Problem, we must learn again that men are unique, capable, and responsible creatures and that commanding officers can thus be trusted. With that trust, our skippers will no longer be muttering under their breath, "Get off my back, sir. I can hack it." And they will hack it.

Editor's Note

In the months that followed the publication of Commander Mumford's article in August 1977, a lively discussion developed in the pages of *Proceedings'* "Comment & Discussion" feature and lasted for more than a year, proving that the issue was (and may still be) a very real concern, both for those holding command and those affected by it.

The debate commenced in December with three letters. In one, a lieutenant agreed with Commander Mumford and offered some anecdotal evidence that he was not alone in his assessment. In another, a chief petty officer also weighed in with his support as well, emphasizing the restrictive nature of directives. But a lieutenant commander was less convinced, providing some of the reasons for both the perception and the reality of the problems cited and then offering his own proposed solutions.

Lieutenant William R. Cooper, U.S. Navy—Bravo for Commander Mumford! His perceptive and professional article is a superb example of the kind of dissertation that makes *Proceedings* a worthwhile investment. I am sure that numerous officers, particularly at the senior levels, will take vigorous issue with his hypothesis. The fact is, however, that everything in the article is true. Numerous commanders, commanding officers, and executive officers I spoke with have acclaimed the article as a direct hit on a basic reason that the Navy is not "fun" anymore. I sincerely hope that all professional members of the naval service—enlisted and officer—read the article and then do some hard thinking and personal examination of their role in the Problem. One may be sure that, if queried in the right manner (perhaps anonymously), a vast number of COs and XOs will support the viewpoint of Commander Mumford. The remaining question is: "Can the community overcome the inertia inherent in the Problem or will we ignore it and hope it goes away?" {Comment and Discussion. *Proceedings* (December 1977)}

Chief Operations Specialist Marcus J. Vooten, U.S. Navy—I fully agree with Commander Mumford's dissertation.

I am in particular agreement with the discussion of directives from above. So often I hear the complaint, "My subordinates have no initiative." As long as *directives*, instead of *general guidelines*, are issued, initiative will continue to be stifled at all levels of the chain of command.

Will the community overcome the Problem, or do we continue to develop *paper-mania*? {Comment and Discussion. *Proceedings* (December 1977)}

Lieutenant Commander Charles R. Cramer, U.S. Navy, Patrol Squadron One—I agree with the premise that over-control of commanding officers will adversely affect morale, retention, professional development, and combat readiness. But, the deciding factor most affecting these parameters of military success is the leadership demonstrated by the CO himself.

Perhaps the patrol squadrons are blessed with particularly enlightened leaders, but I think that they reflect a Navy-wide command attitude best expressed in the words of one of my ex-COs, "Don't be so busy watching for nits that the elephants walk by."

When I returned to the fleet after an exchange tour I found that those "controls" which I was initially so suspicious of were, in fact, guidelines resulting from years of trial and error. They were good, sound management practices to assist the COs.

If Commander Mumford's observations do correctly represent a serious problem in our Navy, I suggest two explanations. The first is communications. Our ability to monitor unit performance and our ability to exercise control from remote locations are nearly instantaneous. In light of the extremely lethal and complex defense problems we face today and the increased degree of accountability to civilian overseers, it is possible to understand why increased stick and rudder orders may be necessary, or perceived necessary. The second reason for increased supervision is more embarrassing: lack of adequate fleet performance. As long as weapon systems continue to be misused or underutilized we can expect to feel a firm hand on our shoulder.

The solution to the real or apparent problem seems to be threefold: first, appreciate the problem of accountability which our seniors face; second, use the communications channels to advise superiors if you feel your prerogatives are being infringed upon; and finally, do your job better. {Comment and Discussion. *Proceedings* (December 1977)}

Editor's Note

The following month (January 1978), an aviation commander weighed in with a number of specific frustrations experienced by aviation commanding officers, one of which dealt with the skipper's handling of disciplinary problems.

Commander L. R. Canepa, U.S. Navy—Commander Mumford's penetrating article gets right to the heart of the issue of crisis management.

Since the article was "surface navy"-oriented, I would like to mention a few items that encumber the commanding officer of an aviation unit. Shortly after a pilot-caused accident, especially if personnel negligence is involved, a new raft of "how to's" and "no mores" is issued. This response is usually caused by an overreaction to pressure put on the squadrons by seniors. Why not "hold" the negligent party accountable rather than further restrict the rest of the operational units?

[...]

In legal matters, the CO must answer to many seniors for how he handles common disciplinary infractions. Why not trust his judgment? He was carefully screened for this assignment and most likely is the best "expert" on discipline problems in his command.

And finally, destroy all "To Be Opened By CO/XO" rubber stamps—the titles are commanding officer and executive officer, not mail yeomen! {Comment and Discussion. *Proceedings* (January 1978)}

Editor's Note

Then in February, a former destroyer XO further endorsed the Mumford article with a rather lengthy comment (here edited down) that drew some comparisons to other federal bureaucracies and included a recommendation to bring in outside consulting help. Commander Jones also provided some additional thoughts on the "Management by Objectives" (MBO) approach to command that had been discussed in the original article and was in vogue at the time.

Lieutenant Commander Robert Drake Jones, U.S. Navy—As a former executive officer in a Pacific Fleet destroyer and a doubting member of the present Navy shipboard management system, I took heart reading the perceptive former commanding officer's article. Unfortunately, the "means/ends" inversion is so widespread today as to be the unspoken governing policy by which entire fleets and the Navy, in general, are managed and led. Commander Mumford, I believe, accurately pinpoints the source of this weak and wasteful management policy—aptly dubbed "The Problem"—as our inability to judge the performance of officers.

In our attempts to use air-tight, justifiable methods to judge officers we have created a system that rewards "procedures," not "goal achievement." In some cases, we have slipped the "goal" over to the "procedure" column, and, now, we have difficulty distinguishing holes from doughnuts. We convince everyone—mostly ourselves—we are judging goals when in actuality procedure is being judged.

Like Commander Mumford, I cannot put my finger on the one defining cause for our evolution into this judgmental abyss. Perhaps he and I are too busy chopping wood to notice we are using a hammer instead of a sharp ax.

[...]

Author [Richard M.] White (also, a successful business consultant who heads a consulting firm) writes [in his book, *The Entrepreneur's Manual*, Chilton Book Company, 1977] he has proven many times that the employee efficiency of a small organization can be increased to 10–15% by the logical and consistent application of the battle-scarred but well proven principles of management by objectives (MBO)! This is a minimum of a 20-fold increase in effective employee efficiency!

But, wait a minute! The Navy *has* MBO! The *Regs* say we *must* have it to pass the admin inspections. Wrong, again, unfortunately! We have something we call MBO that is roundly praised on board ship for several weeks after our human resources management availability, and just as quickly evaporates as the first wave of pre-MBO style, crisis management orders sweep the ship just prior to the next important inspection. Shipboard personnel included in the management team are quick to fall back on the old tried and tested ways to get things done quickly at the first serious signs of major externally stimulated crises. The shipboard managers cannot get over the first major hurdle of MBO, implementation, because they have little experience in this management system and there is little real support from higher up to get it rolling. Why? Because implementing MBO on a lasting basis produces failures and mistakes that can be and are used in our judgmental process of officers' performances. The more daring the management plan, the greater the number of failures, but the rewards of a daring management plan that works are so enormous that the failures are surely worth the effort.

There is no doubt MBO produces superior results in a profit-oriented system. But, the ship's captain can't very well stand at the brow at liberty call and pass out ten-dollar bills to deserving crew members as rewards for superior performances. This harried individual must work to reward his crew in more subtle ways—and his avenues to do so are increasingly limited by our "procedure" versus "results" inversion used to judge his performance. What can we do to get our ships' management teams working on an achievement- and goal-oriented basis?

We can lift our ships out of the clutches of the "average bureaucracy" category and insert them into the lean, hungry, goal-oriented "small firm" class by reducing unnecessary external controls designed (consciously or unconsciously) to provide mental "nails" on which superiors can comfortably hang judgments of officers' performance. Unnecessary external controls make a 250-man crew a lock-step member of the 100,000-man bureaucracy by requiring standardization of procedures to prevent embarrassing (but minor and inconsequential) failures which reporting seniors, as humans, may find difficult to forget at fitness report writing time.

In order for us to sleep better at night (i.e., without the teeth-gnashing induced by recalling the long-haired sailor in the greasy dungarees who didn't salute), we must "lock-on" to the philosophy of judging the ship (i.e., the CO) by her achievements as related to her list of written and approved goals. Forget the minor failures! Judge the overall results! Give the captains (*et al.*) room to "move and shake" as they are supposed to do and as they can do! Judge, reward, and share innovative management anywhere it may be found!

[...]

We have given MBO official and unofficial lip service long enough. Everyone, recruit to admiral, must now be shown the benefits of allowing individual thinking and action (with its mistakes and failures) in the shipboard management arena. It will not be easy, but the choice of whether to make management by objectives really produce significant results or not is almost out of our military grasp. The next voice we hear questioning our shipboard management system could be the often fiscally unfriendly Congress speaking through our civilian Department of Defense leaders. {Comment and Discussion. *Proceedings* (February 1978)}

Editor's Note

The following month brought yet another comment—this time from a retired Navy captain—who went on at some length (here edited) to discuss various points in Commander Mumford's article, concluding with his observation on the power (or lack thereof) of financial remuneration.

Captain K. G. Schacht, U.S. Navy (Retired)—My guess is that the numbers of supporting letters from Commander Mumford's contemporaries will be far outnumbered by critical letters from his seniors. But, his article is honest and probably far more accurate than will be believed by the typical dissenting reader.

[...]

Commander Mumford's suggestion to control the men's pay rates goes too far. A small coterie in the Navy holds to the theory that via money you can get a man to put up with almost anything: long hours, poor working conditions, and excessive family separation. This approach has not worked. Studies have shown that family comes first, working conditions next, supervision third, and money fourth.

In closing, I salute first the editorial board for publishing this article. Second, I extend congratulations to Commander Mumford for the skill, thinking, and courage shown in submitting what is bound to be a somewhat controversial, albeit valuable piece of writing. {Comment and Discussion. *Proceedings* (March 1978)}

Editor's Note

In April, a captain in the Norwegian Navy informed *Proceedings* readers that Commander Mumford's observations "seem to be accurate and relevant" and "are valid for the Norwegian Defense Establishment as well."

13 "COMMAND AUTHORITY AND PROFESSIONALISM"

CAPT James F. Kelly Jr., USN

Discussion of Captain Mumford's article quieted down for a time, but then in August (a full year since "Get off my Back, Sir!" first appeared), *Proceedings* published a new article that addressed the Mumford article directly and stimulated a new round of discussion. In this article, written while the author was in command of the guided-missile cruiser *Fox*, Captain James Kelly postulates that Mumford's observations are either valid or that there is something wrong with the command selection process.

"COMMAND AUTHORITY AND PROFESSIONALISM"

By CAPT James F. Kelly Jr., USN, U.S. Naval Institute *Proceedings* (August 1978): 26–32.

Few articles in recent years have precipitated so much discussion within the sea-going community as the celebrated "Get off my Back, Sir!" which appeared one year ago.* That the author's views caused some concern among a number of

---

* Commander Robert E. Mumford Jr., USN, "Get off my Back, Sir!" U.S. Naval Institute *Proceedings*, August 1977, pp. 18–23.

senior naval officers is, perhaps, putting it mildly. At least one fleet commander in chief was concerned enough to solicit comments on the article from his officers in command of ships and aircraft squadrons. Of those responding, 73% did not agree that, as commanding officers, they were harassed or overly directed by seniors in the chain of command. Only 10% reportedly agreed totally with the article, and the remaining 17% agreed in part.

These are reassuring statistics, perhaps, particularly in view of nagging complaints—which increased in frequency during the Zumwalt years—that command authority was being eroded. But were the proper questions asked in the first place, and were the responses valid and objective? Since it should be reasonable to expect that commanding officers are candid and forthright in their advice to seniors, let us assume that most of the responses were straight from the heart in this instance. "Harassment," however, is rather a strong term and few commanding officers are, in my opinion, likely to experience anything like harassment from their seniors. Even if some of them perceived it, the urge for career survival at least would tempt them to avoid putting their immediate seniors on report to a common senior. In short, many may have told the boss what they thought he wanted to hear.

It connotes a certain sense of insecurity for an officer in command to admit to feelings of personal harassment. He may, nevertheless, feel harassed by the system of checks, double checks, and triple checks which we have established to keep officers in command from fouling up. Perhaps we really did ask the wrong questions or phrased them poorly. "Stifled" and "over-directed" may have been more appropriate terms. Even so, fully one in four of those responding perceived a degree, at least, of harassment and over-direction and was gutty enough to say so. A figure of 25% is not insignificant, and the causative factors should be carefully explored. Further surveys of attitudes should, for the sake of validity, seek anonymous responses to carefully selected questions.

Having enjoyed my recently concluded second tour in command at sea just as thoroughly as my first, I considered Commander Mumford's observations initially with the greatest of skepticism. I have not felt "harassed" by my seniors. There is, however, little question that I and many of my colleagues in command today often feel stifled and frustrated by over-direction and inundated with overly detailed and massive written directives, programs, systems, inspections, workshops, and assist visits. In my view, these combine to downgrade our role from that of military leaders and managers to something approaching the status of local agents for higher authorities, charged with carrying out their programs and philosophies. Too frequently, little or no latitude is permitted with regard to methods employed in reaching the directed objectives.

Commanding officers of cruisers and destroyer tenders report directly to cruiser-destroyer group commanders. Since they do not have squadron commanders, their chain of command contains one less echelon than is normally the case. Owing to the over-extended span of control of their immediate superior in command, they enjoy a certain degree of autonomy. Skippers of destroyers, frigates, amphibious warfare ships, and auxiliary vessels, however, have a squadron commander between them and the group commander. Many of these more closely supervised commanding officers have privately conveyed to me views similar to Commander Mumford's. This problem has been acknowledged in the past by our fleet commanders in chief, and many welcome initiatives have been put forth to ease it. But the perception at the shipboard level, right or wrong, seems to be that "command attention" is still being invoked to an excessive degree, that too many individuals and shore activities still can directly manipulate a ship's tasking and fortunes, and that the "combat zone" is right there in home waters under the watchful scrutiny of the big staffs. Officers and crewmen are heard speaking longingly of "escaping" to distant duty deployments to get away from the daily inspections and assist visits with their related crises. They would prefer to practice their profession free, at least temporarily, from flap-generating staffs.

I believe that most commanding officers (unfortunately for their crews, not all of them) are indeed enjoying their command tours, are challenged by their responsibilities, and believe that our Navy is doing a reasonably good job in most areas. But all this may be in spite of the over-management we are being subjected to by staff and headquarter echelons.

To be sure, there is nothing malicious intended in this over-direction. Senior commanders do not, as a rule, wish to harass officers in command nor do they, I believe, derive any pleasure from doing so. The burdensome directives and time-consuming inspections and checkoff lists are not engineered by people who want to punish the ships and squadrons. They are intended to help, but they reveal a depressing lack of confidence in the ability of a commanding officer to achieve objectives and standards without a detailed blueprint and list of instructions, spelled out in "Dick and Jane" detail. I have heard flag officers say in response to complaints regarding the number, complexity, and frequency of inspections, "Convince me that commanders will do what they are supposed to do and I'll cut down on the inspections!" That is a devastating indictment of our command selection process. If that kind of stick is necessary to get those in command to do their jobs properly, then either we are picking the wrong people for command or we are not producing enough of the right kind of people. Command selection being as stringent as it is, one might conclude that we are stuck with selecting officers for command who need to be kept in line by continued inspections and assist visits. It is a depressing thought.

It is further argued, in defense of the status quo, that junior skippers, because of their relative inexperience, need all the guidance they can get. This view is even more alarming since we are willing, in the meantime, to trust them with the lives of several hundred crewmen and a multimillion dollar ship. If valid, this view also suggests that we should reexamine our process for selecting officers for command.

Do we really need all the people, shore activities, and staffs which we still maintain to ride herd on our diminished fleet, or are these activities, consciously or unconsciously, expanding the workload in order to justify their existence? Has the Navy become so technical and complex that we really do need more supporting activities than ships? Even if the answer to the latter question is "yes," do we really need to spell everything out to the commanding officers— presumably the very best people our officer personnel distribution and selection system can come up with—and then monitor their adherence to direction constantly? If the answer is again "yes," then I believe we are in serious trouble, not just because of an inability to rely on our current commanding officers or to develop ones we can rely on, but because we can no longer afford the massive manpower costs of our vast network of staff echelons and shore establishments. We have been repeatedly criticized by Congress and the Department of Defense for an overly layered and complex staff system. In spite of the streamlining and consolidation of headquarters staffs in the early seventies which resulted, inter alia, in the combined surface warfare type commands, we are still top-heavy and vulnerable to further cuts as the manpower price tag keeps climbing. Many of our staffs are simply too big, and there is clearly too much deadwood residing in some of them. Entire activities and individual billets within activities which do not contribute directly and meaningfully to the support of ships and aircraft must go. We can't afford the overhead anymore.

The attitude seems to prevail among most staffers and many seniors that the commanding officer simply cannot be trusted to get the job done on his own volition. They appear to think that if his feet are not held to the fire, he will fail to achieve the desired objective. This is unquestionably perceived by many commanding officers, and it is highly distressing. This attitude also tends to diminish a commanding officer's self-confidence, aggressiveness, and, hence, his effectiveness.

Consider the magnificent privilege represented by the exercise of command. Right from the instant he says "I relieve you, sir," the captain, regardless of rank or seniority, receives the unquestioning loyalty of the great wealth of human talent constituting his crew. He inherits awesome and absolute responsibility for a multimillion or billion dollar warship and extensive equipment and weapon suites of immense power and complexity. He is treated with no small amount of respect and reverence within his command, but it often seems to end there. He is, occasionally, treated downright shabbily by staffers and by shore activities, particularly if his actions or requests cause them inconvenience or extra work or if, heaven forbid, he fails to follow prescribed methods and procedures.

Further, there appears to be no limit to the number of organizations and individuals who are somehow empowered to tell him how, when, and in what order to do things. Many of them appear to have liberal charters to caution him, direct his attention to, inspect him, "assist visit" him, and so on. Many of the "command attention" items which may engage him and a considerable number of his key people for hours or days are not even coordinated by a scheduling authority. Consequently, scheduling conflicts arise which may cause frantic efforts by the "can-do" captain and his crew to satisfy all of these uncoordinated demands.

He is preached to in countless directives, briefings, meetings, and news-letters, often repetitiously. Many of these have the force of directives (not to be construed, of course, as relieving him in any way of his responsibility). He is lectured by everyone from the force chaplain to the master chief petty officer of the world. He is advised to have special advisors, with direct and privileged access to him.

His constant reaction to excessive, often conflicting, and usually repeti-tious direction from outside his command and, not infrequently, from outside his chain of command, is in vivid contrast to his exalted and respected position within his ship or squadron. This is unquestionably perceived by junior officers, and it disturbs them mightily. They observe their captain accommodating to the policy interpretations of junior officer staffers who have their boss's ear and are in a prime position to make much mischief for the ship, notwithstanding the fact that some of these staffers might not prosper in any responsible ship-board billet themselves. The ship's officers witness their commanding officer fighting and scratching for supply support and repair work and too frequently being forced to accept a shoddy product or incomplete repair.

Recent efforts by one fleet commander in chief to reduce the frequency and redundancy of inspections, certifications, and assist visits have been encourag-ing. A substantive payoff from these efforts, however, is still eagerly awaited at the shipboard level. The number of scheduled and impromptu inspections still constitutes an unrealistic burden. My ship had no fewer than five different aviation certification inspections in a period of four months, each by a differ-ent organization with a differing interpretation of standards which themselves were inconsistent. An all-too-familiar staff response to this common complaint is that without numerous inspections, ships will simply not maintain the requi-site standards. Staffs, however, cannot even agree on the standards. In one case, engineering guidance received from a fleet training group differed markedly from guidance received shortly afterward from the 1,200 psi mobile training team during my ship's preparation for one of its operational propulsion plant examinations (OPPE). In several instances, guidance received from one mobile training team in phase I training was inconsistent with guidance received from another team in phase II. In numerous areas, neither team appeared certain regarding what the propulsion examining boards would actually accept as standards, suggesting it was largely dependent upon the personal whim of the persons constituting that particular board.

Some inspections lose meaning as "gamesmanship" is applied. Having been through refresher training at least a dozen times, it has become difficult for me to take parts of it completely seriously. You hold your feelings in check as you are told by some young officer what a basket case your ship is. Then, through some miracle of advanced training technology and patient skill on the part of the training group staff, your progress shoots upward until, happily, you pass the battle problem with flying colors, thanks to the unselfish efforts of the instructors and staff and the enthusiasm of your crew. ("They're green, Captain, but they have the right attitude!" Of course they have the "right attitude." You threatened to hammer the first one of them who disagreed with an instructor, right or wrong!) Your young officers and junior petty officers perceive this lack of candor, and many find it offensive. (The more experienced ones, having been through it before, are already resigned to the routine.) The only redeeming part of it all is the abundance of otherwise scarce training services which help improve the ship's readiness in spite of instructors who may not understand much about your particular equipment configurations and capabilities.

I have never received an unsatisfactory grade in a major inspection, but I am almost convinced that such accomplishments involve as much luck and gamesmanship as skill. I believe that many commanding officers live in mortal fear of failing inspections or examinations, notably OPPEs, because of the possible career consequences. What has become of the lofty purpose of the 1,200 psi propulsion improvement program? Never intended to be a hammer over the commanding officer's head, it was designed to further the worthy objective of operating our ship propulsion plants with greater safety, reliability, and efficiency. Many staff and shipboard personnel now seem to view a mobile training team visit as a crash course in how to pass an OPPE, complete with detailed instructions on how to impress the examiners, e.g., clean, starched dungarees, shiny shoes, polished brightwork, highly stylized repeat-back rituals, etc. Many of our young people view this part as pure and simple "Mickey Mouse" when they know that much of this showmanship is abandoned as soon as the examiners depart and that it contributes marginally, if at all, to efficient, safe propulsion plant operation.

A ship which is soon to deploy or about to undergo an OPPE or INSURV (material inspection and survey) enjoys the greatest of support from staffs and maintenance facilities at the 11th hour for correcting conditions which may have existed for months. Correcting these deficiencies was no less important months ago than it is now for safe, reliable, and efficient propulsion. Ah, but the stakes are different now and the staffs, having a vested interest in the outcome, feel the heat. Consequently, carte blanche authority is granted to turn on the repair facilities in a frantic attempt to fix everything when it may be too late. Yet, ships are told that they create their own crises by starting preparations too late!

The primary thrust of inspections should be to identify problems, not culprits. If we could temper the all-too-prevalent staff view that inspections are failed and casualties incurred primarily because of command mismanagement or inattention, we will go far toward restoring confidence in and among commanding officers and improving performance. All ships of a class are not created equal. Some have built-in problems which good management alone cannot correct. In this regard, it is clear to me that junior officers and petty officers feel rather overwhelmingly that we seniors have failed miserably to provide adequate resources for the support of our ships and equipment.

The temptation to look for shipboard culprits at any sign of failure is common to most staffs and, having served many years on staffs, I can understand the reasons why. It is, of course, a self-defense mechanism. Its guidance is certainly lucid enough, the staff reasons, and, heaven knows, all agree that it is ample enough. The staffer reflects upon how well he performed when he himself had command of or served in a ship of similar class, and it becomes very tempting to generalize about poor shipboard planning, weak leadership, and other similar conditions best solved by firing someone. Many highly placed seniors now tend to judge skippers of today by their own prior experiences in command. It is not a valid comparison. Many flag officers of today can look back with justifiable satisfaction on four or five tours in command. In stark comparison, today's "successful" surface line officer is fortunate to have two. The commanding officer of a guided-missile destroyer, for example, is more than likely serving in his first shipboard command. Moreover, he is likelier than not to have fewer than six years of experience at sea.

When many of today's flag officers commanded that same guided-missile destroyer, it was a new ship and, not infrequently, their second or third command— a "bonus" for previously demonstrated excellence. We had no operational propulsion plant examination in those days. No propulsion examining boards. No mobile training teams. The salient objective was meeting commitments, never mind that the propulsion plants were operated under conditions which today would be considered manifestly unsafe.

It should come as little shock, then, that one in four commanding officers today feels harassed. What disturbs me most, however, is that other officers are vaguely uncomfortable in command. I firmly believe that some of them wouldn't be there at all if there were some surer, less risky route to promotion. I am convinced that many think of their command tours primarily as stepping-stones to greater things. They probably speak in public of the joy of command because that is what they are expected to say. Down deep, they may wish to get out from under before the whole thing falls apart.

The average number of years of prior sea experience among first-tour commanding officers is decreasing alarmingly. Bonus commands for super performers are few and far between. Rather than using and reusing our best and most proven officers in command in "follow-on" tours, we are whisking them through command tours at a dizzying pace and moving them on to bigger and better things ashore in spite of the fact that our ships, sensors, and weapon systems are becoming more and more complex. We assign aviators—hard-charging and intelligent to be sure, but relatively inexperienced in ships at sea—to command sophisticated amphibious warfare and mobile logistics force ships. We do so in order that they may get their tickets punched for aircraft carrier commands, all because of the quaint notion that only aviators can successfully command the latter and also because of the need to provide command opportunity for aviation captains.

We appear to be attempting to train everyone to be flag officers. We are building careers, not seagoing professionalism, in our Navy today, and it is, in the view of many, beginning to show. Like most others who are concerned with the eroding image of command, I have a prescription for curing this condition.

First, we must take whatever measures are necessary to increase experience levels in officers being ordered to command. Multiple command tours should be increased and we should re-tour proven captains in command billets. Moreover, command and executive officer tours should be lengthened to three years. Two years simply is not enough time to influence the incumbent in command regarding the long-range impact of his policies and decisions. We must, of course, accept a concomitant decrease in command opportunity, but the taxpayers, who pay the whole bill, deserve nothing less than ready, reliable ships, commanded by the best of the proven professionals who are comfortable, confident, experienced, and capable in command. Accepting a reduction in command opportunity will, to be sure, generate monumental morale problems unless we make other routes to senior rank more promising and credible. It will make the screening and detailing process more difficult, but the good of the Navy and the nation must be the paramount consideration—not morale and not some notion of what constitutes an ideal and balanced career.

Second, we should seek to restore confidence and authority in those serving in command by minimizing over-direction. We should put stringent new controls on the issuance of directives. It would help to limit the number of commanders empowered to issue directives to ships. Directives should be signed by flag officers or other senior commanders only. They should avoid detailed directives on how to achieve the desired goals unless standardization is dictated by safety, security considerations, or by federal law. The term "command attention" should be restricted to unusual, nonrecurring situations of grave importance. Its overuse has seriously diluted its effectiveness. Every inspection, exercise, or task need not be preceded by a form letter from someone telling the commanding officer to get ready and to get personally involved. Staffs should rarely or never require ships to submit programs of action and milestones (POA&Ms) unless they are absolutely needed for the staff's own effective planning. The POA&M

is properly the command's internal management tool, designed to facilitate its own planning effort. It should be used as a device for the ship to monitor its own progress in moving from square A to square Z—not as an excuse for staffs to try to force ships to plan properly.

We should avoid stifling commands with ever increasing requirements for standardized programs to implement and cycle through and permit those in command more leeway in achieving the desired goals. It is time now to ask ourselves if all commands really need such time-consumers as human resources availabilities. Is the substantial amount of time and manpower now being devoted to them really making a commensurate contribution to the Navy's mission? Beyond the highly practical and concrete personnel qualification system (PQS) and preventive maintenance system (PMS), how many standardized systems/programs are really necessary? How much does some of the current effort spent by commands in generating inspection-proof records contribute to sea control? I recall being taken to task once during an inspection for an admittedly tedious and cumbersome internal instruction on training. Never mind that there was ample evidence of effective training being accomplished. Never mind that 88 of 95 crewmen who had taken the most recent advancement in rating examinations were advanced and that our qualification board process was producing excellent results. The issue appeared to be that we were not following our own internal directive! *Gotcha!*

We should take visible steps to improve the prestige of commanding officers. I have heard some rather silly methods for doing this proposed over the years. One involved a scheme for paying "responsibility" pay. Money for this purpose would be a sheer waste of defense dollars. There is no shortage of officers seeking command, so why waste the money? What is needed is greater faith in their judgment and resourcefulness by those serving in staff echelons. Let the commanding officer share in policy formulation at the staff level. Invite his presence and comments at staff meetings and make those meetings something more than mere recitations of the latest no-nos. Unit commanders should consider their commanding officers as ex officio members of their staffs rather than relying so heavily upon the less experienced junior members of their personal staffs.

Many commanding officers, I am sure, would view this as an added burden, but I am frankly disappointed by the lack of access to flag officers that ship captains normally have and the infrequency with which flag officers consult commanding officers.

Finally, we should set the record straight that ships and aircraft are more important than staffs and shore activities and that most of the latter exist to support the former. Staffs should do less direct monitoring and more supporting. A staff is something to be leaned upon, not beaten with. To avoid the abuse of delegated authority, we should put strict limitations on the power of staffers. Too many sins are committed in the name of the admiral or commodore. Ships have had their reputations impugned or their proficiency in certain areas questioned because of vindictive staffers who had disagreements with ship's personnel. The ship commanding officer may not even be aware of the bug put into the boss's ear by his staff expert, much less be given the opportunity to rebut it. I have witnessed this more than once while serving on staffs and in flagships, and I am convinced that it is still happening.

The perception of officers currently in command toward these problems is probably of only passing importance. Officers in command of ships and aircraft squadrons have always chafed under the management of staffs. What is important, however, is the perception of junior officers and the effect of those perceptions on career decisions and upon their own command aspirations. Also important, of course, are the views of our senior staff commanders. If they honestly feel that the current degree of direction, guidance, and supervision is appropriate, then I believe that a serious lack of trust and confidence in the ability of officers selected to command—the very best the system can produce—is indicated. If this is the case, and it may be, then we had better undertake an earnest effort to improve professionalism in command by increasing tour lengths and re-touring proven commanding officers.

Perhaps we truly do need a wet/dry Navy.

Editor's Note

Two months later, an aviation lieutenant commander responded with a proposal for changing the Navy from a "rules orientation" to a "goals and participation orientation."

Lieutenant Commander Kevin M. Smith, U.S. Naval Reserve, Officer in Charge, Light Photo Squadron 63, Detachment One—Captain Kelly succinctly identifies a number of impediments to effective management within the Navy and recommends solutions that should be given serious consideration. The [...] problems cited by Captain Kelly, Commander Mumford, and others indict the present management system and profoundly point up the requirement for an in-depth analysis of our management concepts and philosophy.

However, once the management problems have been identified, there is an unfortunate tendency to treat the symptoms instead of the cause of the malady. An example of this is one author's recent recommendation to issue a directive to require a reduction of directives. This proposal sounds logical, but is, in fact, specious, since it merely attacks the symptoms and will ultimately accomplish nothing. The problem of too many directives is not caused by the absence of a directive limiting directives. The problem lies in the existence of a rules-oriented organization whose prime orientation is management by domination.

The Navy exists today as a rules-oriented organization. On the surface this does not appear to be a malady; after all, without rules, we would have anarchy. Upon close inspection, however, we discover that a rules- and domination-oriented organization is inconsistent with any viable human resources program and, more important, incompatible with management by objectives. In addition, such an organization is characterized by a distinct lack of member participation; ideas are not solicited, and therefore, the members' feelings of contributing to the betterment of the organization are negligible.

But can an organization as large and complex as the Navy leave its rules orientation and become truly objective oriented? I believe it can.

The objective-oriented organization is specifically referred to as the human resources model. This model assumes that man needs to work, is happy when working in a meaningful job, and will continuously seek responsibility. This model also recognizes the dignity of the individual and that the success of the organization depends upon the collective inputs of all its members. Decisions in this model are made at the lowest possible level and true decentralization is a reality. This model strives for high levels of job satisfaction and recognizes its investment in human resources. These resources are never squandered, and a manager who unreasonably sacrifices human resources for mission accomplishment is either reeducated or fired.

This organization is not only more capable of adapting to change, which is essential in conducting warfare, but new solutions and innovations are all but guaranteed. Changing the Navy from a rules orientation to a goals and participation orientation will not be easy, but there doesn't seem to be any other way to solve our severe and perplexing management problems. {Comment and Discussion. *Proceedings* (October 1978)}

Editor's Note

This new round of discussion—begun by Commander Mumford's article and now sustained by Captain Kelly's—continued with a focus on the problem of too many inspections. A master chief serving on the staff of the commander of Naval Surface Forces, Pacific, not only pointed out the problem but proposed a rather detailed remedy. The solution proffered has lost much of its relevance through the passage of time (procedures and problems have changed), so it is omitted here, but the basic premise for the discussion remains relevant as commanders should heed the cry for reduced oversight as born not out of laziness or sheer iconoclasm but out of a legitimate concern for efficiency and enhanced fleet performance.

Master Chief Sonar Technician Jim Bussert, U.S. Navy, Commander Naval Surface Forces Pacific Staff, Maintenance Coordinator Center—Captain Kelly's excellent article highlights the fact that when you participate in conversations on the mess-deck, in the chiefs' quarters, or in the wardroom, you find one common area of shipboard agreement that bridges the first-termer/career and officer/enlisted gaps. It is the frustration of the endless 12-month inspection each year that constantly disrupts planned work. Ashore, the squadron and type commander schedulers are equally frustrated in trying to find ships which are materially able to get under way and do not have numerous inspection visits already scheduled.

The executive officer of an amphibious transport dock (LPD) told me he counted 75 inspections from one deployment to the next. What then is the situation for a guided-missile cruiser (CG) with additional antiair, antisub-marine, nuclear-capable, and engineering inspections?

Editor's Note
Master Chief Bussert then laid out a revised approach to the inspection cycle—too dated for inclusion here.

This proposed 11 months of self-sufficiency may sound like heresy in today's Navy, but the constant paperwork, visits, and crises are driving our desertion rate up and morale down, without producing any noticeable improvement in material condition and readiness. Under this proposed schedule, the initiative, pride, and resourcefulness of the officers and enlisted men should bloom. There would be time for urgent repair work, and routine maintenance, housekeeping, and training could be realistically planned. [. . .] The command may ask for help or assist visits during this test, but soon the tendency would be to hack it once the umbilical cord is broken, rather than have an outsider come in and do one's job. It used to be that way when a sailor fought if someone slandered his ship's name. It was called Navy "can-do," and it can be that way again if we give our men a chance to grow into it. Instead of 12 months of crisis management, let us have one month of crisis and eleven months of management. {Comment and Discussion. *Proceedings* (November 1978)}

Editor's Note
The following month (December 1978) saw another comment that included some observations regarding the consequences of excessive oversight.

Lieutenant Commander Charles H. Gnerlich, U.S. Navy, Executive Officer, Navy Recruiting District, Philadelphia—Congratulations to Captain Kelly! I have heard it said more loudly, more profanely, but never more accurately. There is something wrong in our chain of command; it is not just a perception.

Today's commanding officers are not always well qualified, and are almost never completely trusted. And even if the lack of trust, qualifications, and experience were just staff and junior officers' perceptions and not fact, the treatment of today's COs by staffs, seniors, and directives makes the perception fact.

And if, as Captain Kelly states, one in four of our COs admits to feeling harassed, what percentage are hiding their feelings from themselves and from their seniors? And what percentage of their subordinate officers and crew senses the lack of trust and feels their skipper is being picked on? A CO, who is always directed and helped, tends to look for direction and help when it is not needed, and he certainly does not inspire subordinates in the way that he might if he had experience and reasonable control of his own ship's internal evolutions. . . . {Comment and Discussion. *Proceedings* (December 1978)}

Editor's Note

The following March, one officer (Lieutenant Commander Brian J. Barry, USN) challenged some of Master Chief Bussert's assertions regarding the inspection cycle (adding some proposed solutions of his own), and the following month another officer (Lieutenant Commander Bruce K. Johnsen, USN) took the opposing tack. The latter cited an example of a cruiser that "was assisted and inspected into a lowered state of morale and operational readiness," but was able to effect a major transformation for the good once she was sent to a forward-deployed station, away from all the "help." He concluded his comment with: "I know that Chief Bussert's concept of minimizing the numbers and compressing the time frame of inspections will result in growing operational readiness, improved material condition, and high morale. I've watched it happen!" {Comment and Discussion. *Proceedings* (March 1979)}

14 "ELEMENTS OF COMMAND: SELF AND FAMILY"

(Selection from chapter 11 of *American Admiralship*)

Edgar F. Puryear Jr.

This portion of one chapter in Edgar Puryear's *American Admiralship* explores the role of the Navy spouse. Not too surprisingly, Puryear found that there is a difference between Navy spouses and those of the other services.

"ELEMENTS OF COMMAND: SELF AND FAMILY"

(Selection from chapter 11 of *American Admiralship: The Moral Imperatives of Naval Command*) by Edgar F. Puryear Jr. (Naval Institute Press, 2005): 551–71.

I had the good fortune in doing the research for this book to visit many times in the homes of numerous admirals. I had the same opportunity to visit the homes of the Army and Air Force generals I had interviewed for my book *American Generalship: Character Is Everything*. To my surprise, I observed a contrast between families of the respective services: there was a very special relationship in the marriages of the Navy families I visited. I learned that the challenges of family life were greater in the Navy than in the Army or Air Force. One of the major differences was that a naval career involved constant separations because of sea duty. While members of today's Army and Air Force now experience similar separations because of America's worldwide commitments as a superpower, members of the Navy have always faced this challenge.

In a personal interview that took place in April 2002, I asked Adm. Thomas H. Moorer to describe the role his wife had played in his naval career. He replied:

A few months ago I received the Naval Academy's Distinguished Graduate Award. I reviewed a full dress parade by the Brigade of Midshipmen. I made a speech. They kept telling me I always talk too long. It was Parent's day, so the mothers and fathers were there. I talked to them about how important it was to bring to the Academy [young people] with the [right] mental, moral, and physical qualities.

Then I turned to the midshipmen and told them I had stood where they were standing and I thought I knew what they were thinking. "You are wondering why the admiral doesn't shut up and sit down." I said to them, "I just have one more thing to say, so hold onto your rifles a little longer. What I want to talk about is marriage in the service. My wife and I moved twenty-five times during our career. We have four children, ten grandchildren. I just want to talk about my wife. She has always supported me. She has never complained. I want everyone in this audience to realize if it wasn't for my wife, Carrie, I wouldn't be standing here today." What a special tribute to a great lady.

Admiral Moorer reminisced about his marriage: "We had this prohibition on getting married prior to the end of two years. So shortly after I commenced flight training, I did get married on Thanksgiving Day of 1935. It was a long-standing romance that had been going on for years. I think I had my first date with . . . Carrie when she was about thirteen years old."

Asked if his wife supported his decision to go into aviation, he said: "She had been very wonderful about that. I know that many, many wives discouraged their husbands from going into aviation at that time. It was far more dangerous than it is today, primarily because of material failures. I mean the equipment was not nearly as reliable because, of course, at that point it was under development in many areas. So many wives discouraged their husbands, but mine had never discouraged me at anything that I set out to do. She never even commented on it.

Adm. Arleigh Burke's (CNO 1955–61) marriage may or may not be typical for naval leaders. I discuss it in detail here because it was a partnership worth emulating, one that provided support for both partners throughout their Navy life together. Burke was introduced to his wife, Roberta "Bobbie" Gorsuch, by his Academy roommate. Burke was a big, blond Swede; Bobbie was only five feet tall and weighed less than one hundred pounds. They courted throughout his four years as a midshipman and were married on June 7, 1923, Graduation Day.

Burke was stationed in Long Beach right after their marriage, and the only quarters they could afford was a furnished apartment in San Pedro, not at that time a particularly nice neighborhood. But they wanted to be together. His initial assignment was on the battleship *Arizona*. Shortly thereafter he was assigned to Torpedo Training School in San Diego, and although it was only a four-month course, Bobbie went with him. They always tried to stay together in spite of their limited funds and the difficulty of finding a place they could afford.

Once, out of loyalty to the *Arizona*, Burke bet on his ship's crew in a rowing contest with the crew of the *Concord*. The *Arizona*'s crew lost, and Burke lost the funds he had set aside for Bobbie's living expenses. He owned up to what he had done in a letter, and she wrote back to say that he had done exactly what he should have done and that she had taken a job to tide her over until payday.

After they had been married four years, Burke was assigned to a school in New York. Between the two of them they had only $120 to last until payday at the end of the month. All they could get in the way of quarters was a rented room so small there was not even space for a chair. Often, all they could afford to eat was doughnuts. At the end of the month they had only $2 left. In spite of the financial challenge, both described this time "as among the happiest of their lives."

Separations were frequent during Burke's early career. On his first assignment in World War II he wrote to Bobbie every day, mailing his letters whenever the ship was in port. They were separated for two years during the war, but still they both corresponded almost daily. He always provided as full a description of the battles he was involved in as the censors would allow.

When Burke was assigned to Norfolk after World War II, Bobbie rented a small apartment, hoping to see more of him. She didn't. He was given a demanding job that required him to go to work early and stay late. Bobbie met him at the dock at the end of each day. One of his colleagues, Don Griffin, recalled, "Arleigh Burke's wife would come down to the dock to pick up Arleigh and take him home. She would drive up, park her car on the dock. Sometimes she would sit there until eight or nine o'clock waiting for him to come down."

Chapter 5 described how Capt. William R. Smedley warned Burke to get out of town quickly because Secretary of the Navy Forrestal wanted Burke's help in writing his memoirs, a job that would take him away from sea duty. As soon as he received the warning, he called Bobbie and asked her to pack. He left the building he was working in and met Bobbie, who was waiting for him in their Dodge with all his gear. At Westover Airfield he managed to find an outgoing cargo flight and went out to the car where she was waiting. "I think I've got a way out," he told her. "I'll get my baggage and you shove off for Washington." So off she went on a five-hundred-mile trip in the middle of the night, alone except for their Great Dane and with no place to stay along the way.

Burke's next assignment was as commanding officer of the *Huntington*. His ship was suddenly detailed from the Sixth Fleet to make goodwill calls on the east coast of Africa and in South American ports. He was gone for a considerable period. When the ship returned to the Philadelphia Navy Yard, Bobbie was there to meet him, having rented a furnished apartment even though they would have only a month before he returned to sea. They did not have even that long. He received a telephone call on his arrival ordering him to the Pentagon "without delay," so they left before dawn, driving straight to Washington.

When they arrived at the Pentagon, he jumped out of the car and dashed inside. E. B. Potter's biography of Burke describes what happened next: "Bobbie waited. And waited. This sort of thing had happened many times before. No telling when Arleigh would be out. It was up to her to find a motel where they could spend what was left of the night. . . . And to serve notice of eviction on the tenants to whom they had rented their home. Bobbie had dedicated her life to looking after Arleigh, and willingly so, but there were moments like this when she felt her allegiance to the Navy slipping."

The separations and long workdays occurred throughout their career. Potter noted that Adm. Thomas H. Moorer was among those who recognized her contributions to Burke's career.

Bobbie was so gentle and unassertive that few people discerned the vital role she played in her husband's career. Moorer, however, through his long association with the Burkes, recognized that Arleigh, in any circumstances a great man, was a greater one thanks to Bobbie's advice and support. She was his steadying influence, cheering him out of his glooms and restraining his impulsiveness. He consulted her on all matters, social, professional, and administrative. She lacked his technical training and his broad, hard-earned knowledge, but she was unusually gifted with patience, common sense, and inner strength, and she devoted herself unstintingly to her husband's needs.

On August 1, 1967, Admiral Burke retired after six years as CNO. The secretary of the Navy at the time was John B. Connally. While the secretary sent Burke the normal congratulations and praises for his contribution and achievements, he sent him a special note as well:

Dear Admiral Burke:

When a man achieves greatness, he is almost always backed and aided every foot of the way by a wonderful and devoted wife. It is beyond my official powers to award Mrs. Burke the decoration she so richly deserves, however, I want to say that you have been most fortunate in your wife's choice of a husband.

To Mrs. Burke and to you, may the best of everything be yours for many years to come.

A Navy wife can have an enormous effect on her husband's career. A wise commander, as Arleigh Burke was, realizes that and takes it into account. When Admiral Burke was selecting his staff as CNO, he looked beyond the job candidates:

I didn't choose the staff. I'd tell the Marine Corps that I would like to have a Marine aviator, a lieutenant colonel with these qualifications. Send me one. I finally learned to talk to the wives before I made a final decision. The wife's attitude toward the service—what she believes her husband's duty to the country is—that's a very important factor. If she believes her husband has a tremendous duty, he does, too. Never, though, when the selection process got down to where I was talking to a wife, never once did she fail. I had six years there and a staff of maybe fifty people and they were a high-performance staff.

I asked Admiral Holloway to describe the role his wife played in his success. He told me:

I think I had the talent to have made captain on my own, maybe rear admiral. But . . . I would never have gotten beyond that stage without her. One of the things she did is she kept me from getting into trouble. I might suggest I was going to do something and she would say: "That's the dumbest thing I ever heard. If you do that, you will just look stupid." She was very tough-minded, especially about not letting me get a swelled head. She brought me down to earth repeatedly.

Also she was so solid at home during the long deployments. The other wives tended to congregate at our house, not for bridge parties, but for reassurance, support, and just companionship. If they had a problem, they came to her. "Dabney, what should we do?" It just seemed natural for them to do it because they had such respect for her judgment. They would go to her for advice.

Regarding his flying, he said:

She knew it was dangerous. She knew because the two of us had to so often call on a pilot's wife to break the news that her husband had been killed in a crash. When I was CO of VA-83 on the USS *Essex* cruise of West Pac with the Seventh Fleet, two of the four squadron commanders were killed in landing accidents coming aboard the carrier. When I was XO of VF-52 during the Korean War, both my skipper and my wingman were shot down. I know Dabney was concerned, but she did her best not to show it. Dabney has always been very good at being able to handle things like that.

She knew it would just be another worry for me to worry about her. I'm only finding out now how she felt about the long deployments. At the time, she never let me know it. I only found out two or three years ago how much it bothered her, how tough it was for her, particularly during the Vietnam War, when I had two successive Christmases away from home.

My aircraft went down twice in Korea. She knew about it. Her response was, "You promised you'd be careful." She accepted the fact that as a career naval officer I was flying F9Fs [a jet fighter] in combat in Korea. She could not help but know that the casualty rate was between 20 to 25 percent for the pilots, but this never came up.

Our second daughter was born when Dabney was by herself out on the West Coast. I was in Korea. My mother came out from Washington, D.C., by train to be with her when the baby was born. She got another Navy wife to take her to the hospital. I didn't see my daughter Jane until she was five months old.

On *Enterprise,* I was gone both Christmases to the Tonkin Gulf for the war in Vietnam. Those things were pretty tough, but never a whimper from her. It was so important for me to get encouraging, positive letters from Dabney. There was never any hand wringing. If the allotment check was late she didn't tell me about it. If the children were sick she didn't tell me about it. She did indicate she wished I was home and that she missed me and that the children missed me. She accepted my being gone as part of my American duty and not just as a career naval officer.

When Holloway had the opportunity to enter Admiral Rickover's nuclear program, he asked for Dabney's input. She knew how demanding it would be, but her answer was, "That's your decision." And when Admiral Holloway became CNO, his wife was expected to shoulder a huge burden too.

There was something that was very bothersome to me. Mrs. Zumwalt and Dabney knew each other long before I became CNO. Mrs. Zumwalt told her, "Now, you, of course, are going to be responsible for all of the wives in the Navy. We've already organized the naval officers' wives clubs, to organize and give guidance to the enlisted wives' clubs." Dabney said, "I don't think Jim would be in favor of that."

When she told me about the conversation I agreed, "You're absolutely right. We're going to stay completely out of what the wives do. That's not our business. We're not going to organize the wives. If they want to do it themselves, that's one thing. We will do all we can to keep them informed and to help them find housing and take care of their families. But we will do that officially through individual commanding officers, base housing officers, and the Navy and Marine Corps Relief Organization. Navy wives' clubs should not have an official role but help as needed in referring . . . spouses in need to the proper officers' organization designated to take care of their needs and then provide any help that a support group can in terms of morale and understanding."

Adm. Stansfield Turner, who headed the CIA during the Carter administration, pointed out some of the difficulties for a Navy spouse:

My first wife, Patricia, . . . was with me through the CIA and a couple of years after. She did an excellent job. . . . In the Navy, you have a greater sense of family, because the wife is the commanding officer of the wives when the ship is overseas. The wives who have problems tend to go to the commanding officer's wife. That puts a great strain on the wife because for six months she's mother and father. It's difficult for a group of women to be stranded when their husbands are three thousand miles away. It makes for a family environment in the Navy more than it does in the other services.

Admiral Trost spoke of his wife's role in his career:

I would say [it was] considerable. She would say none, but I would say very considerable. First of all, when you are deployed, the wife becomes dad, mom, and everything else. When I left Charleston, South Carolina, as commander of the nuclear sub *Sam Rayburn* to go on patrol [in] December 1968, I sailed down the river and waved to my wife on the bank over at the officers' club with my little kids standing there. It wasn't easy. It was just before Christmas, and I would not be home for Christmas. Our ship would be on patrol for seventy days.

I particularly think of her and the hardships when I was the executive officer of the *Scorpion,* a submarine that was lost five years later. At the time we had deployed quite a bit. I was on the ship for nineteen months, and we were deployed for more than half the time. We were in and out all the time. So my wife was suddenly also faced with being the mother confessor for wives whose husbands were on the ship as well as for everybody else. It is a tough responsibility. She tells the story about the time when one of the young enlisted wives called and said, "Mrs. Trost, I am sorry to bother you, but I have a washer problem." Pauline told me, "I said to myself, have I run into a blood bath?" She asked, "What is wrong with it?" And she said, "It doesn't run." Pauline asked, 'Well, what kind is it?" It was a Sears brand, and my wife said to herself, "Thank God," with a flash of inspiration. And she said, "Call Sears. That's what I would do." She had a lot of responsibility, and . . . she had confidence in her ability to handle the challenges,

and although she didn't seek it, she was superb. We are not social but-
terflies by any means, but she is one of the better diplomats that this
country has ever had.

...I think we had twenty-eight or twenty-nine moves in a total of
thirty-six years, some of them just six-month tours of schooling, like
going to New London for a ... six-month submarine school, Then I
went back to New London for six months for nuclear power training.
My family went with me. Then, I went to Idaho for six months of
nuclear prototype training, and we had other six-month moves, and
relocations of that nature. The wife is critical through all of this. I
would say I was especially fortunate with my wife because she did a
wonderful job. The nice thing about it is that I am going back this
afternoon because I would rather be with her than not be with her.

I discussed the role of the wife with Admiral Hayward, who agreed that a
supportive spouse is an important element of a successful naval career.

Certainly I would endorse those statements of Admiral Moorer and
Holloway on the role of the wife. We lived in a generation in which
marriage as an institution was founded on an admiration from both
sides, male and female. Not that many of our age group are still with
wives and ... married for years and years—I'm coming up on my fifty-
fifth. Loyalty and shared commitment are a built-in part of our character to begin with, a calling for a strong team effort, and you know
it's going to be for the rest of your life. That is so very important and
helpful to the durability of a partnership.

There are two ways to look at the wife's role, first when the officer
is a junior officer, the other is when he is a senior officer. The roles
for the wife are quite different in each circumstance. When I was a jg
to lieutenant ... I went on two cruises to Korea, eleven months each
time [1950–51]. Long cruises, with two young children left behind.
Think of it. You have this young wife with two very young daughters,
... providing basically the whole family support since her family was

on the East Coast. Alone, Peggy managed to deal with all the sickness, car trouble, the plumbing, and the rest of that, at the same time worrying about whether she was going to get her husband back; and we lost a lot of guys. Because of our relationship and my confidence in her strength, I was able to do my job without having the burden of worrying about what is going on back home. Same thing occurred in Vietnam. I had a different level of responsibility at that time. I was a commander and then captain. I went to Vietnam first as an air wing commander, [then] commanding a deep-draft ship. Then I returned soon after that as the commanding officer of the USS *America* [a conventional carrier]. If you consider the overall time spread of those three commands, I was gone a lot of the time when my children were in junior high and high school. Vietnam attitudes were developing rapidly, the early drug scenes were upon the country, civil rights were active. It was a very tough time. In looking back on that time, I am in awe of how incredibly the wives held their family together and did a great job. They deserve a medal that none of the men would have deserved. They provided tremendous support.

. . . When I was Seventh Fleet commander, CinCPac, and CNO, Peggy's role became much more diverse and enjoyable at a time when our children were on their own. We shared a lot of interesting travel, meeting important people, with Peggy's role much more directly support. . . . Additionally, by meeting with other wives [and] helping to find [out] things not self-evident to me she played a crucial role, . . . keeping [me] . . . advised as to what is really happening. . . . Wives are truly important to helping you do your best. I can't imagine doing an acceptable job with no wife, or enduring trouble at home. There was never a time when Peggy ever tried to influence me to leave the Navy.

Admiral Kelso pointed out:

You've got to remember when we deploy, the wife's at home. She carries all the load. When I go off to sea, she's got four kids to take care of, and most of the time she couldn't even reach me because we didn't send the kinds of communications that we have today. We are much more lenient with communications today than we were then. So the wife plays an absolutely necessary role in your career. I would never have been able to do the things I did without her being willing to make my life a happy one at the same time she was taking on both roles when she was home. That was not easy, particularly with teenage boys.

I asked Admiral Kelso how he met his wife.

That's a long story, but it's a good story. Once a year her family visited my hometown, sometimes more often than that. My dad would say, "You ought to go see that pretty little girl." I never had anything to do with her. . . . I was home for Christmas my freshman year at Annapolis, and my dad made me get out of the car and go see Landis. So I did. That started a long romance. We dated from about the second year on. She came to Washington when I was a junior and senior working for a congressman, and she supported me in a style that I've never forgotten.

They were married a week after graduation. "We've been very close since then," he said,

. . . but in my early career, we were away as much as we were home, so when your children are young, it is very difficult. I don't think you can find very many successful naval officers who do not have a wife [who supports] their career. There may be one or two. The wife provides so much support to you, particularly if you have a family. You can hardly survive without her. A young mother always wants to take care of her children, but a Navy wife must become father as well, and often how children feel about the father depends on what the mother/wife tells them when he is gone. She provides enormous support to the wives of the personnel on the ship when their husbands are deployed. In many cases she is the one who is called for support by the other wives. Normally she spends an enormous amount of time doing that. Without her blessing . . . it is pretty hard to have a career in the Navy. In other words, if it is unacceptable to her, then the officer, or sailor, is not going to be very happy. Because under the circumstances you are consistently being pulled in two different directions. Many wonderful officers have to leave the Navy because the wife cannot accept his career. They don't want to separate and lose their wife. The role of a wife is so important in a Navy career. . . . By the time an officer is selected to be a three- or four-star admiral, the function of the wife is very visible. I don't mean she makes him an admiral; he earns the stars, but he is unlikely to get there without the strong support of her and the Navy.

You sort of put a lot of things together in an officer's career—is he healthy? Is he competent? Does he have a stable family situation? All those things play into the total equation. I can't emphasize enough how important it is to have a wife who accepts his career and supports him. In my case, Landis always knows how to keep my hat size the same. The stars with my children are always on her shoulders.

Admiral Johnson spoke of the many moves his family made as his career progressed and how they affected his family.

I think Garland, my wife, would say the same thing. It got harder with every deployment, not the other way around. People say, hey, you know, you get used to it, it gets easier as you go. I don't think so. Garland's got this written down at home because she used to—in her *Joy of Cooking* cookbook, in the back cover—write down every address we ever had. It was either twenty-six or twenty-seven in thirty-two years. We had one child, our daughter. I think she handled it very well. But it was tough. We spent a lot of time apart. There's a part of me that regrets that, but we also understood that it was the business we were in. A lot of what I was able to do in the United States Navy was enabled by my wife. She focused me. She had the great ability to put my head in the right place, center my thinking, and keep me focused. She also kept my ego in check. Reminds the emperor when he has no clothes, those kinds of things. That sounds trite when I say them, but she had a huge impact. . . . I really don't think I'd be where I am today if I hadn't married her. That's how strongly I feel. There's no question about that in my mind. It could be a tough life. We don't need to be apologetic about that, but we also have to be fairly pragmatic. It's tough. We ask a lot of our families, absolutely.

Adm. Robert L. J. Long remembered one of his less pleasant assignments:

I'd have to say my next assignment was somewhat unnerving. I had orders to go as the executive officer of a brand-new antisubmarine submarine, the *K-1*, which, incidentally, President James E. Carter was also assigned to. But then my orders were changed to go to be the exec of *Cutlass*. That boat had gone through two or three skippers in one year and two or three execs in one year. It was a real problem. And it was at Key West, Florida, where there was no real housing to speak of. So we were less than enthusiastic about, one, going to a place where housing was difficult and, two, going to a submarine that was screwed up.

So, anyway, we went and arrived down there, with two babies and no place to live, mosquitoes that almost could carry the children away. We moved into a motel. It was Sunday, so I went down and walked aboard *Cutlass*. All the officers were there, including the skipper, Lieutenant Commander Charles Styer Jr. The officers were all sitting in the wardroom while the exec was reading the deck logs aloud to make sure that they were properly worded. I said to myself, "Well, that doesn't look very good to me." Then I went in to see the captain, who was a very close friend of mine.

He said, "Bob, we're going to sea tomorrow for two weeks, and I'd like to have you go with us." I said, "Captain, I just arrived here. I don't have a place for my family. They're sitting in a crummy motel out here. I'd prefer not to." He says, "Well, I really want you to go. We'll make some time available to you when we get back."

I was so mad, I went back to the motel, sat down, and wrote out my resignation from the Navy. I said, "If this is the way the Navy treats its people, I don't want any part of it." Fortunately for me—or maybe unfortunately—my wife, Sara, got on the telephone to her father and told him, "I don't think Bob should do this." Her father was a guy I really respected, a great guy, and he talked me out of it. He said, "Hey, this is a temporary thing. My observation is that you are ideally suited for the Navy. You have a lot to offer. Don't let this one incident destroy that." So, anyway, I went aboard.

Adm. Kinnaird R. McKee, who succeeded Adm. Hyman Rickover in 1982 as head of the Naval Reactors program, said of his wife:

She was part and parcel to everything I did. It was she who encouraged me—I'll tell you a story about that. I met my first wife and we became engaged very soon after that. When we told her mother that we were engaged, she said, "that's fine," or words to that effect. Didn't register a lot of emotion. But the next morning at breakfast, she sat down with her daughter—my fiancée—and said, "You've got to be sure you really know what you really want to do, because that young man knows what he wants to do, and he knows where he's going to go."

Admiral McKee pointed out a historical precedent for the Navy wife's role:

Daniel Boone's wife, Rebecca, shared his life for fifty-six years. She gave him ten children, and grieved with him when two were killed during his campaigns. She could mold bullets, shoot a flintlock, and skin a deer. She spent much of her life alone for long periods of time, not knowing if her husband was alive or dead. Submarine wives would fit an updated version of that description. They don't mold bullets or shoot a flintlock, but they still have to carry the load alone, for long periods of time—and still they do not know. They have to be just as talented and independent as their men. And they are—I know that better than most. They share the same commitment and accountability, and nobody has a bigger stake in the outcome.

Admiral McKee's wife was the sponsor of the USS *Louisville* (SSN 724) in 1985. He made the principal address, then turned to her and said, "I can't find the words to say more, Sweetheart, except that none of what has been credited to my account would have been possible, or would have had any meaning, if I had not been able to share it with you and with our children."

The wife of a successful career officer must be just as selfless as he is. Adm. Charles R. Larson said that his wife "had to give up her own career and her own life, really, to totally support me. I guess one of the problems with making admiral as early as I did, that was just about the same time the kids were getting ready to go off to college, where she could then go and do her own thing. She really ended up pretty much doing the things that she needed to do to support me, particularly when you consider seven years at the Naval Academy, where we've got social events at least five nights a week, and then eight years as a four-star."

I noted to Admiral Larson that traditionally, Navy spouses have endured longer separations—and the added responsibilities these entail—than other service spouses. He agreed: "I think the Army and the Air Force started learning this lesson during Desert Storm, what it's like to have people gone for six months, because they really were not used to it; even when they went to Europe, the families went with them. So they never experienced this. My wife spent a tremendous amount of time as kind of a representative of the wives when we were gone on deployments. The wives of the senior officers had a more important leadership role."

Among the most interesting experiences I had in writing this book were my several interviews with Adm. Paul David Miller. He had a remarkable career and retired as a full admiral after twenty-eight years of service. I asked him what role his wife had played in his success. He responded:

> Ah, bless her heart. Lots. She still does it today. I do very little at home. She takes care of all the finances at home. She raised the boys more than I did because I was gone so much. She comes from a small town in Illinois. She didn't know what she was getting into, but if you asked her, she wouldn't change a thing. She handled the deployment, the long and frequent separations brilliantly. She's a beautiful lady, and she was an outstanding representative of this nation. The NATO people loved her. She was able, particularly while the boys were growing up, to never permit them during the long absences to lose touch. We were still a family even though we were apart. She had them write little notes on her letters to me. I responded to everybody. I have stored away some of the things they said.
>
> The Navy today is so much different. We stayed in touch with Colby [his son on active duty in the Navy] in the Persian Gulf with e-mail almost daily. We would get pictures of him every couple weeks about what was going on on the ship. It made the deployment go a lot faster.

Admiral Miller commented that he loved what he was doing in his naval career so much that he rarely took leave. I asked him if his wife ever complained about that. "Complain is probably too strong a word," he answered. "She handled it and moved forward. I was unable even when I was in command to ever leave it. She would tell me that every time I was at home that my mind was worried about something aboard ship, every time."

Leadership and command can be very lonely, particularly in wartime, when tough, agonizing decisions must be made. Admiral Burke's daily correspondence with his wife, mentioned above, filled much of the vacuum and loneliness and helped give him the strength he needed for command. In his biography on Nimitz, E. B. Potter made the point that when Nimitz assumed command in the Pacific, "he felt the loneliness of high command, for nobody in the Pacific theater could share his appalling responsibility." Actually, that is not quite true; he could and did share it with his wife. He received a great deal of support from her in their correspondence during those lonely times. As the war developed, he shared many of his thoughts with Mrs. Nimitz in his correspondence, particularly personal and personnel matters. His letters to her were as important as hers to him because he could tell her things he could tell no other person.

In October 1942, a time of crisis as U.S. forces were involved with the recapture of Guadalcanal, he took the time to tell her about a dinner he had on October 16 with the governor of Hawaii, and on October 21 he wrote about a popular speech he had given at the University of Hawaii, sharing with her: "At least a number of people came to compliment me." One letter written in September 1942 referred to a personnel change involving Vice Admiral Towers. Mrs. Nimitz knew that her husband did not approve of Towers's methods, so he "hastened to assure her by letter" that "I am to have a new air advisor. Never mind. We will get along fine."

While, as I noted in chapter 6, Admiral Nimitz initially retained Adm. Husband Kimmel's staff when he assumed the post of CinCPac in December 1941, he gradually rotated them out. But he did that only after sufficient time had elapsed to expunge the stigma of the surprise attack on Pearl Harbor. In addition, he believed in regularly reinvigorating his staff with officers fresh from combat and wanted to give his own staff a variety of experiences, particularly sea duty and combat. He shared another reason with his wife: "My staff will gradually change from those I found to those I choose." When Nimitz had to relieve Vice Adm. Robert L. Ghormley, a friend of many years, as commander, South Pacific, he shared his doubts with his wife: "Today I have replaced Ghormley with Halsey. It was a sore mental struggle and the decision was not reached until after hours of anguished consideration. I hope I have not made a life enemy. I believe not. The interests of the nation transcend private interests." Nimitz also enjoyed passing on good news. He had received a letter from Secretary of the Navy Frank Knox telling him, "all of us here are very proud of the way you are handling your job." Nimitz wrote to Mrs. Nimitz: "Good news. Perhaps I can last out the year."

Adm. Raymond A. Spruance also knew the loneliness of command and leaned on his wife, Margaret, for support. His correspondence with Margaret throughout their long separation in World War II was vital to his well-being. In February 1942 he wrote to her, "I need my wife to keep me cheered up. . . . Life has certainly lost its interest for me since you left, and the worst of it is that I have no definite date to look forward to when I shall see you again." Always careful not to violate censorship, he had a clever way of keeping her informed. For example, when Halsey's activities were written up in *Life* magazine, he suggested she read it, knowing, of course, that it covered his activities too.

Spruance's thirteen months as Nimitz's chief of staff were, he wrote to his wife, "an inspiration . . . and I hope watching him has taught me more patience and tolerance. He is one of the finest and human characters I have ever met, yet has all the energy, courage, determination, and optimism that is needed in a great military leader." Another letter told her: "My staff has been working up to midnight every night and I have been working during the day, but I refuse to go on the night shift." Admiral Spruance kept Margaret informed of his daily activities; with the planned invasion of the Gilbert Islands looming, he told her she would not hear from him for several weeks because "I shall be too occupied with the other matters to do any writing." He unloaded to her his contempt for the press: "Everyone in the country seems at liberty to express his opinions on the strategy of the war and to publish his ideas to the largest audience that will listen to him." Social events were a necessary part of his activities as a commander. "At times like this and at social events when names fail me I need you very badly," he wrote.

As the war intensified, he told his wife how much her letters meant to him. "My letters will be irregular from now on, but keep writing regularly yourself. Mail will reach me at intervals and it means a great deal to me to hear from you." When he received notice on February 10, 1942, that he had been promoted to full admiral—at age fifty-seven the youngest man to reach that pinnacle—he wrote: "Getting this rank was something that was beyond my utmost expectations." As the war drew to an end and assignments of flag officers were being determined, he told Margaret that he would be happy to replace Nimitz as

CinCPac. "Don't ask me where I would have my headquarters, or what I would be able to do about you, for I don't know yet. I am in favor of our high command getting back on board ship during peace, so as not to lose touch with the fleet. You know well enough that wherever I may be, I want to have my family near me. I know you must be disappointed over this, but you know my feeling that a line officer must be willing and anxious to go to sea and to remain at sea. So just be patient for a while longer and wait and see what happens."

Children are, of course, an integral part of Navy families. Children and parents have mutual responsibilities toward one another, and the relationship often involves selflessness and sacrifices on both sides. Among the memories of Rear Adm. Chester W. Nimitz Jr., son of the great naval leader, are some that provide insight into the family life of naval officers.

> Dad had probably the most highly developed sense of duty, as a public servant, and devoted himself first, foremost and always to that aspect of his life, and perhaps secondly to his wife. I believe the children were a natural outgrowth of marriage, and . . . my guess is that his basic belief . . . was, the children were expected to perform and conform and enhance the stature of the family, and so long as they did and were not delinquents, really, that was pretty much the responsibility of the father. . . . Dad was . . . away a tremendous amount of time, so that when he did come home, all of us children understood absolutely and instinctively from our mother that by golly, we made the time he was at home relatively [quiet]—he'd contest this, I'm sure, but by our lights it was relatively serene. It was far more serene than when we were with Mother alone.

Asked about his father's role in the home, Chester Jr. responded:

> Let me say in the first place, Father was a completely dedicated naval officer. I think such leadership and influence as he did exert in the home, and mind you, in the days we were brought up it was certainly largely an upbringing by the mother because the father was away a

good deal of the time, his method was simply the same method he used everywhere else, to express sublime confidence in the dedication and right thinking point of view on the part of his children and of their understanding of the almost necessity of doing well at what they undertake. It certainly was not a close personal kind of a, this is the way you do things because in the long run that's the way you succeed. It was a considerably more formal sort of standard setting. I really think that the Navy consumed an extraordinary percentage of his thoughts and energies.

Admiral Nimitz's daughter-in-law, Joan, provided further insight into the driving force in his life. It was not money, she said, but service to his country and his beloved Navy. She commented: "I remember that when he retired, I'm sure that Chester's mother hoped that he would do something to occupy himself. Here he was, just full of energy and ability and good mind and everything else. He wouldn't take a business job of any sort. He was totally disinterested in finances or money. He never handled any of the money in the family, you know. Mother did all of that. And he didn't care about money at all, so he didn't want a job for money, and he didn't feel that he could take a sort of a commercial type of job."

Flag wives fill an important leadership role in their relations with other Navy wives, but they can also play a role in the development of the junior officers. Adm. James F. Fife was a junior officer under Admiral Nimitz before World War II. During that time Admiral Nimitz's wife offered genuine family hospitality to him and to other junior officers. "For many years Mrs. Nimitz used to say that she brought me up," he recalled. "This was later on, after [Nimitz] was chief of naval operations in Washington, and I've always had very proud feelings that she would feel that way and would say so . . . she had a great influence on my whole career." She did an excellent job. Fife retired as a full admiral.

The following remarks from Admiral Holloway reiterate the importance of the spouse's role in a naval officer's career, particularly as the officer moves up the command hierarchy.

The influence of a wife on the career of a naval officer can be enormous. I have never known an officer to be promoted to a position of responsibility on the basis of his wife. Yet I am aware of many situations when a naval officer—particularly in the grades of captain and above—was not given a favorable assignment or even failed for selection because of his wife. This unfortunately has occurred because the wife has had a drinking problem or even a personality conflict that has made her an embarrassment when appearing publicly with her spouse. I don't say that these cases of a woman ruining her husband's career are common, but they are not infrequent, based upon my experience as a senior officer sitting on selection boards and as the chief of naval operations responsible for the appointment of all flag officers in the Navy.

That's the negative side of the picture. What about the positive? A Navy wife can be an asset to her husband, and this influence is exerted almost entirely through her relationship with her spouse, not in lobbying other senior officers in his behalf. That latter activity is an absolute taboo, and almost inevitably results in almost fatal problems to the person she is trying to help. I can say from experience that senior officers do not like to hear about . . . [a] subordinate's professional competencies from that subordinate's wife. It is obviously totally subjective and generally does nothing but plant the seeds of suspicion in the mind of the senior that the couple is attempting to hide something.

The good Navy wife endures separations and accepts the additional burdens of doing her job as homemaker and the husband's job as "paterfamilias" without a complaint, at least to her husband. She has the children always seeming in good spirits and well-mannered whenever the husband returns from one of his long sea duty jaunts. There is much more to being a good Navy wife than simply accepting with stoicism the vicissitudes of the service. It takes leadership on their part as well.

After reporting what senior naval officers have had to say about Navy wives, it seems only fair to approach the subject from the wife's point of view. The wife of a senior admiral talked about what she considered to be the most difficult part of being a naval officer's wife. Let her remain anonymous, because she spoke for many wives.

My husband was a naval aviator, a carrier pilot, and during his flying days there were special concerns. First was the constant threat of a fatal accident. Had we not lost so many close friends and classmates in crashes, I might have been able to put it out of my mind. But then when I had almost forgotten that ever-present danger, we would get the news of the loss of another friend. It didn't help when the men brought home the aviation safety magazine. It had all of the brutal statistics. Flying off a carrier was listed as the most dangerous profession going. But our guys loved the flying, so I just had to be fatalistic and not think about an accident happening to my husband.

The long deployments were also a problem, especially when the children were still at home. They missed their father and never quite understood why he had to be gone so long. Actually it wasn't the separation that bothered me the most; it was the fact that the more days he was gone on a carrier, the more chances he had to get killed. That's where so many losses seemed to occur. On almost every cruise a squadron would expect to lose one or two pilots in crashes. . . . When my husband stopped flying, the deployments weren't so bad. I missed not having him around those months, but I was sure he would be coming home, an assurance I did not have when he deployed in a squadron.

There was one other aspect of being a naval aviator's wife that was difficult, and for me, unanticipated. We had to share our men with the squadron. I hadn't realized the intense camaraderie that exists in a squadron where everyone from the skipper on down is risking his life every day together in this very dangerous profession. As the squadron gels during the re-forming phases after each cruise, with a new commanding officer and replacement pilots, the spirit becomes intense. The pilots are competing in air-to-air combat with other Navy squadrons, and winning an intersquadron competition means everything.

Happy hour was the biggest headache for the wives. After a full day of flying, the pilots from each squadron would gather at the bar of the air station "O" club and get pumped up, singing squadron songs and holding arm-wrestling contests with the other squadrons. I guess in current jargon that is known as male bonding, but I wanted my husband to come home and help me with the kids. Of course, about half the squadron were young, unmarried, and pretty happy-go-lucky. They had no families to go home to. So all too often, the whole bunch would transfer the party to the home of one of the senior officers when happy hour broke up. So as a skipper or exec's wife, I did get my husband home, but with a half a dozen starry-eyed but hungry young ensigns and jaygees who had to be fed and nurtured. So it was scrambled eggs or carryout pizza and Chinese for dinner after feeding the kids and putting them to bed.

The admiral's wife added,

Don't underestimate the pull of the squadron camaraderie. The night before deploying to the Korean War, the squadron held a "beer muster" at the . . . local watering hole, and even the married pilots showed up—with their wives. I know the same thing happened during the Vietnam War. It was virtually a ritual for the pilots who were deploying to combat to bid the noncombatants goodbye in a raucous farewell party. I didn't understand it at the time, and it was sort of hard to take. I understand now that it is part of the role of being the Navy wife.

INDEX

responsibility, 68; execution of, 55–56; fitness for, 51; fundamentals for success in, 53; indoctrination by, 57–60; loyalty and, 64–67; morale and, 63–65; organization by, 56–57; preparation for, 53–55; teamwork and, 62–63; training by, 61–62; usurping province of subordinates, 66–68

Hobson, 10

Holland, William J., Jr., 31–37

Holloway, Dabney, 166–68

Holloway, J. L., III, 10–11, 37, 166–68, 181–82

honor, 123–24, 126

Horne, F. J., 91

Hornet, 99, 104

Human Resource Availability, 130, 142

human resources model, 157–58

humor, 48

independence: of COs, 11–12; focus on procedures vs., 129–30. *See also* autonomy; flexibility in command

Indianapolis, 108

indoctrination, 55, 57–62, 66, 69

information flows, across commands, 18

initiative, 117–18, 137

innovation, 47, 130, 137

inspections: administrative, 136, 147–48; gamesmanship and, 151–52; reducing number of, 158–59, 160; of ships, CO and, 149–50

instructions, 71–73, 80, 128–29, 147–48. *See also* micromanagement; over-direction

INSURV (material inspection and survey), 152

integrity, admitting to a mistake and, 123–24

intelligence, for command decisions, 97

International Law, *Flying Arrow* incident and, 71–72

Isbrandtsen Steamship Line, 71

"I've Got It Made If I Don't Foul Up" commanders, 40

Japan: battle of Midway and, 102, 104; defense by, after Marcus Island raid, 99; defense by, Doolittle raid and, 101; on Leyte Gulf vs. Saipan operations, 107; Perry's orders to open, 35; submarines of, Marcus Island raid and, 97–98

Java Sea, Battle of, 8

John F. Kennedy, 10, 24

Johnsen, Bruce K., 160

Johnson, David and Garland, 173–74

Jones, John Paul, 125

Jones, Robert Drake, 141–43

judgment, 46, 117, 119–20, 130

junior officers: guidance for, 148; Hayward on spouses of, 170–71; on lack of creativity and independence opportunity, 129–30; perception of management of staffs by, 156

Jutland, British fleet teamwork and, 62

Kelly, James F., Jr., 145–60

Kelso, Frank and Landis, 171–73

Kimmel, Husband E., 83, 90, 178

King, Ernest J.: ARCADIA Conference and, 87; as combined COMCINCH and CNO, 91; on COMINCH in relation to CNO, 89; Dec. 1941 orders to Pacific Fleet by, 87–88; on Fifth Fleet Operation Plan, 106; Fletcher's Stewart Island action and, 96; named COMCINCH, 85–86; naval high command and,

ABOUT THE EDITOR

Thomas J. Cutler has been serving the U.S. Navy in various capacities for more than fifty years. The author of many articles and books, including several editions of *The Bluejacket's Manual* and *A Sailor's History of the U.S. Navy*, he is currently the director of professional publishing at the U.S. Naval Institute and Fleet Professor of Strategy and Policy with the Naval War College. He was awarded the William P. Clements Award for Excellence in Education (military teacher of the year) at the U.S. Naval Academy and is a winner of the Alfred Thayer Mahan Award for Naval Literature, the U.S. Maritime Literature Award, and the Naval Institute Press Author of the Year Award.

The Naval Institute Press is the book-publishing arm of the U.S. Naval Institute, a private, nonprofit, membership society for sea service professionals and others who share an interest in naval and maritime affairs. Established in 1873 at the U.S. Naval Academy in Annapolis, Maryland, where its offices remain today, the Naval Institute has members worldwide.

Members of the Naval Institute support the education programs of the society and receive the influential monthly magazine *Proceedings* or the colorful bimonthly magazine *Naval History* and discounts on fine nautical prints and on ship and aircraft photos. They also have access to the transcripts of the Institute's Oral History Program and get discounted admission to any of the Institute-sponsored seminars offered around the country.

The Naval Institute's book-publishing program, begun in 1898 with basic guides to naval practices, has broadened its scope to include books of more general interest. Now the Naval Institute Press publishes about seventy titles each year, ranging from how-to books on boating and navigation to battle histories, biographies, ship and aircraft guides, and novels. Institute members receive significant discounts on the Press's more than eight hundred books in print.

Full-time students are eligible for special half-price membership rates. Life memberships are also available.

For a free catalog describing Naval Institute Press books currently available, and for further information about joining the U.S. Naval Institute, please write to:

Member Services
U.S. NAVAL INSTITUTE
291 Wood Road
Annapolis, MD 21402-5034
Telephone: (800) 233-8764
Fax: (410) 571-1703
Web address: www.usni.org